Farmington
and Farmington Hills

This 1870 view of Grand River, one block east of Farmington Road, was taken two years before the great fire. The large stone structure is O.B. Smith's Drygoods Store, where the fire started. Other businesses shown are Mrs. Pierman's Millinery Store, Warren Selsby's Jewelry Shop, Dr. Woodman's Drug Store, the Dohany building, and Jackson's Blacksmith Shop. Pictured from left to right are: John Hiler, Ack Northrup, Thomas Hanafon, James I. Wilbur, Ben Arnold, William Kennedy, Uncle Fields, and Walker Brown in front of J.N. Power's General Store. (Courtesy of the Farmington Community Library.)

THE
MAKING OF AMERICA
SERIES

FARMINGTON
AND FARMINGTON HILLS

DEBRA ANN PAWLAK

ISBN 978-0-7385-2419-1

Published by Arcadia Publishing
Charleston, South Carolina

Printed in the United States of America

Library of Congress control number: 2002117479

For all general information contact Arcadia Publishing at:
Telephone 843-853-2070
Fax 843-853-0044
E-Mail sales@arcadiapublishing.com
For customer service and orders:
Toll-Free 1-888-313-2665

Visit us on the Internet at www.arcadiapublishing.com

Front cover: *In 1899, more than 30 years after the Civil War ended, local veterans and their wives reunited at Farmington's Town Hall. (Courtesy of the Farmington Community Library.)*

Contents

ACKNOWLEDGMENTS

The experience of researching and writing a history book on Farmington and Farmington Hills has been a welcome challenge. I certainly could not have done it alone. Through the efforts of family, old friends, and some new ones, this volume came together. It all started when my on-line writer pal Vickey Kalambakal thought I should contact Arcadia Publishing with a proposal. Even before Vickey, there was my UCLA on-line writing instructor, Nancy Shepherdson, who brought me into her writer's group and taught me that I could do it. Then my good friend Alberta Asmar of the Walter P. Reuther Library at Wayne State University suggested the obvious—write about Farmington, my hometown.

From there, it all seemed to escalate with local archivist Peggy Brann and the Farmington Community Library, who made their impressive historical collection available to me. Then came personal historian Donna Ellis, who was invaluable with her unique way of bringing old pictures to life. Next I called upon Tim Ostrander, who patiently gallivanted with me from corner to corner of our two cities lugging along his camera and tripod. Not one of them ever complained, but always offered their assistance with a smile.

Thanks also go to my editor at Arcadia Publishing, Christine Riley, who patiently answered my many questions, giving guidance when I needed it, and to my Mediadrome editor Helen Stringer, who gave me confidence in my writing abilities. I also want to thank Brian and Chris Gettel, who so generously volunteered their beautiful home up north on Little Traverse Bay when I needed quiet time to write. I pounded out many of these words on their kitchen table.

In addition to those already mentioned, I must also thank my good friend and the best "do-it buddy" in the whole world, Linda Wells, who helped me with everything from editing to picture organization. I would be lost without her. My sincere thanks also go to Therese Kushnir, another good friend, who lent assistance with all sorts of odd jobs. They never stop encouraging me and always listen to my crazy ideas without laughing. I couldn't ask for more.

I must also thank my family: my husband Michael, who had the wisdom to buy a house in Farmington in the first place; my daughter Rachel, who always keeps me on my toes; and my son Jonathon, whose quiet support spurs me on. While this book has been my challenge, I'm sure that living with me this past year has been their challenge!

Finally, I'd like to express my thanks to the community. I will never look at Farmington or Farmington Hills in quite the same way. Unbeknownst to most, a unique heritage surrounds us. Even though I couldn't cover every single person or event in one book, I tried to hit the highlights. As a result, I sincerely hope that you, too, will see the things around you a little differently, and maybe some of you will be inspired to do some research of your own.

The Owen House is decked out for Governor Fred Warner's campaign in 1904, after he was nominated for a second term. Roosevelt and Fairbanks were also promoting their second term in office. (Courtesy of the Farmington Community Library.)

Introduction

Covering approximately 4 square miles, Farmington, Michigan was founded in 1824. Completely surrounding Farmington is the larger city of Farmington Hills, measuring just over 33 miles square. Strategically located 20 miles west of Detroit and 46 miles east of Lansing, the state capitol, the two cities have been intertwined from the beginning, sharing a rich history, as well as remarkable residents.

Before people moved in, however, there were glaciers. Cutting across Michigan's lower peninsula 12,000 years ago, they etched lakes and rivers along their paths. The local terrain was altered forever, covered with glacial till over 100 feet thick. The rich soil would one day benefit the spirited men and women who settled here.

The first people to inhabit the area came from Siberia. Walking across a land bridge to Alaska, they advanced across North America. Among their descendants were the Potawatomi Indians who lived in Lower Michigan, as well as in Ohio, Indiana, and Illinois. Farmington's three main roads follow their original Indian trails—the Orchard Lake Trail, the Grand River Trail, and the Shiawassee Trail.

The French were the first Europeans to claim the Michigan area. Founded in 1701 by Antoine de la Mothe Cadillac, the city of Detroit was settled on the banks of the Detroit River until the British took over the occupation of what was to later become the Michigan Territory. They were still in control at the start of the Revolutionary War.

Once the fighting was over, officially ending British occupation, the Northwest Territories were divided. Various treaties were made with the Native Americans, forcing them to give up much of their land. The British, however, refused to leave and continued doing business with the Native Americans despite the formal establishment of the Michigan Territory in 1805. As unrest between England and America continued, the War of 1812 commenced and Michigan found itself once again controlled by the British. After the American victory, Michigan remained under military rule until Lewis Cass became governor. Cass firmly believed that Michigan's interior was a valuable asset to the United States.

By 1820, Michigan's Potawatomi Indians were left no choice but to surrender what land they still possessed to the federal government. It was then sold for $1.25 an acre to settlers from the east intrigued by the untamed wilderness. The area west of Detroit where the three main Indian trails met was particularly tempting.

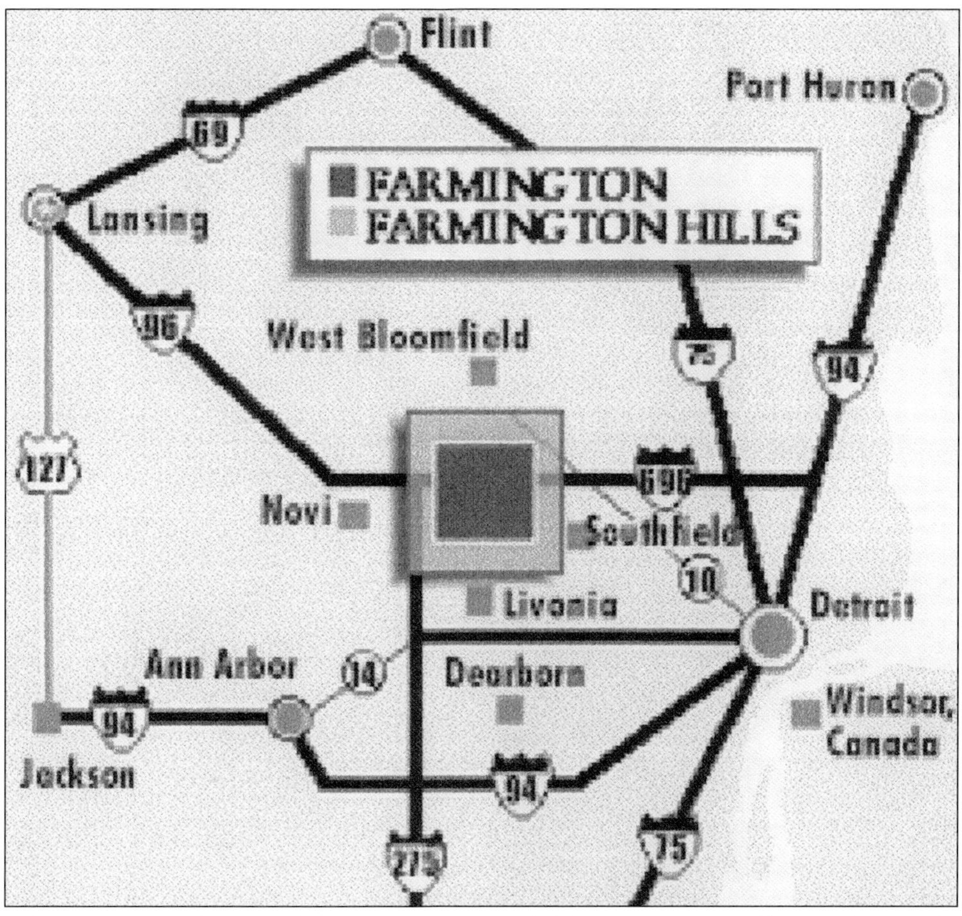

This map depicts the City of Farmington, surrounded by Farmington Hills and other nearby communities. (Courtesy of the Farmington Community Library.)

And so it was that Arthur Power, a Quaker from Farmington, New York, came to Michigan in 1824. Power cleared his land and built a small log cabin—the first such structure in the newly founded village often referred to as Quakertown. As more settlers followed, churches, schools, and cemeteries were established. Soon a bustling community, along with several smaller settlements, evolved.

On March 30, 1827, the Michigan State Congress allowed townships to elect their own officers. Two weeks later, Farmington was recognized as a township and was one of the first to hold an election. Township officials met regularly, passing laws and taking care of local government business.

Nine years later, when the Michigan State Anti-Slavery Society was formed, Arthur Power's son Nathan was one of its 11 vice presidents. With the passing of the Fugitive Slave Law in 1850, it became illegal to help escaping slaves. If convicted, the offense carried a $1,000 fine. Despite the serious risk, the township became part of the Underground Railroad. In addition, many local men heeded the call of President Abraham Lincoln and volunteered their services on behalf of the Union Army during the Civil War.

After the war, 1 square mile of Farmington was incorporated into a village centered on Grand River and Farmington Roads. As luck would have it, Grand River became the main thoroughfare for travelers between Detroit and the newly named state capitol, Lansing. With a stagecoach line regularly passing through, local inns and taverns flourished until disaster struck.

An intense fire broke out in O.B. Smith Drygoods Store on Grand River in 1872. The volunteer bucket brigade ran out of water and the fire rapidly spread down the main road, taking several businesses and homes with it—city offices included. The fire was finally stopped when a house directly in its path was torn down, leaving a gaping space that the flames couldn't jump. It was a devastating blow, but residents rallied to rebuild their community, including a new town hall.

The beginning of the new century brought the Detroit United Railroad (DUR) to town when it named Farmington Junction (the corner of Grand River and Orchard Lake) one of its hubs. For the next 30 years, the DUR dominated the area until automobiles replaced the rails.

In addition to the DUR, Farmington was also home to Michigan Governor Fred Warner, who served three consecutive terms in office. He not only helped shape the state as a new century began, but the entire Warner family played a key role in the development of Farmington and the surrounding township.

The city and the township actively participated in World War I—both on the home front and in Europe. There were war gardens, neighborhood sewing circles, and bond drives. So many local young men enlisted that, in 1917, only girls were present at Farmington High School's graduation ceremony.

Farmington celebrated its centennial in 1924 and officially became a city with its own mayor in 1926. After weathering the Great Depression and the closing of its two banks, the city and the township endured another world war. Once again, local citizens took their role in world affairs seriously as they formed a Defense Council. Heroes emerged and a Japanese balloon bomb found its way to Gill Road not far from the downtown district.

Once the war ended and super highways were built connecting Detroit to the suburbs, the community grew at a rapid rate. Farms turned into country estates, which eventually gave way to subdivisions. In 1951, the mayoral form of city government was replaced by the city manager and council, which still exists in Farmington today. Wood Creek Farms Village, a 1-square-mile residential area, was incorporated in 1957. The following year, the Village of Quakertown was also incorporated and, in 1972, both villages along with the rest of the township voted to become the city of Farmington Hills.

As a new century begins, Farmington and Farmington Hills remain vital communities. With many historic places and a noteworthy past, the two cities offer distinctive insight into decades gone by and, at the same time, welcome future challenges. So, for those of you who think that nothing ever happens in Farmington, think again . . .

1. The Beginning

Farmington's Potawatomi Indians left behind a legend. They told the story of Minnow Pond and its mysterious curtain. They believed that this dark, dense curtain appeared at the end of the trail, making it impossible to know what lay beyond. Some thought it was a thick black cloud falling from the sky, while others claimed it was made of smoke rising up from the many campfires burning in the night. All agreed, however, that when the ominous curtain emerged, no one dared pass through it.

Potawatomi folklore describes a beautiful young Indian maiden in love with a handsome brave. Traveling with a band of Potawatomis one warm summer day, they came to the end of a trail not far from Minnow Pond. While the braves ventured into the woods for food, the women stayed behind preparing the camp. The young girl, engrossed in her work, never even noticed her lover was gone. The young man intended to slay the biggest buck and impress his ladylove.

The brave found his perfect deer grazing peacefully in the grass around Minnow Pond. Cautiously, he approached the animal. When he was close enough, he quietly drew an arrow from his quiver and placed it against the string of his bow. Taking careful aim, he pulled back, opened his fingers, and released the arrow. It soared through the air, stopping only as it struck the deer. Momentarily dazed, the injured animal dropped to its knees. As the young brave approached his victim, the deer suddenly jumped up and ran.

Dropping his bow and arrow, the brave took hold of his hunting knife and gave chase. As the wounded deer reached Minnow Pond, it fell for the final time at the water's edge. The brave carefully moved in to finish the kill. As he raised his knife, the deer gave one last swift kick. The ground broke loose. The hunter and the hunted both fell victim to the pond, lost forever.

Later that day as the men returned to camp, the young girl grew impatient for her lover. She anxiously asked each of the men if they'd seen her missing brave. No one had. As dusk fell, the desperate girl left camp alone in search of him. All night long, she wandered the woods, calling then listening, but no one answered. As the hours passed and night turned into day, her heart felt heavy. Finally, at daybreak, she ventured further into the woods, refusing to give up.

Eventually, she came upon his bow and arrow. Her heart leapt for joy. Next, she found the spot where the deer first fell. From there, the trail was easy to follow as drops of blood, hasty footprints, and broken twigs led the way to Minnow Pond. A short distance from the water, she stopped. There in front of her hung the fabled Potawatomi Curtain. It seemed to fall from the sky surrounding the pond.

Frightened by what lay before her, the young girl screamed and at that very instant, the sun emerged, shining brightly. She lifted her arms and cried out: "Oh Sun! Oh Sun! Pour forth your rays upon this somber curtain! Let them penetrate its darkness that I may see the footsteps of my Indian brave!"

A dark cloud then covered the sun and mighty winds began to blow. The maiden cried out once more: "Oh Tempest! Oh Tempest! Slash this curtain with your breath! Lift its billowy folds that I may see beneath it the footsteps of my Indian brave!"

Rain then poured from the skies, beating fiercely upon her. "Oh, Rain! Oh, Rain! Pour forth your torrents! Wash away this sable curtain that I may see the footsteps of my Indian brave!"

Next, the thunder came almost drowning out the sound of her voice. "Oh, Thunder! Oh, Thunder! Pour down your fire upon this accursed curtain and consume its every fold that I may see the footsteps of my Indian brave, my own true lover."

This image shows the legendary Minnow Pond area today, near Halsted and Fourteen Mile Roads. (Photo by Tim Ostrander.)

This photograph shows the Inner Ridge of the Defiance Moraine at Twelve Mile and Drake Roads. (Photo by Tim Ostrander.)

Lightning flashed and another deafening clap of thunder shook the earth she stood on. The trembling ground gave way and the maiden plunged into the murky waters of Minnow Pond. She finally joined her lover. Together, they now wander through the forests of a happier hunting ground with the ill-fated deer alongside them still carrying the perfectly aimed arrow deep in his heart.

As many as 12,000 years before the Indians spoke of the Legend of the Potawatomi Curtain, the oceans receded from the southern half of Michigan's lower peninsula and the glaciers moved in. Traveling south from what is now Canada's Hudson Bay, the glaciers carved valleys, lakes, and rivers as they slowly moved along. Fortunately, the Upper Rouge River was one such waterway cutting across this area diagonally from northwest to southeast. These rapidly moving waters would one day play a vital role in the establishment and survival of Farmington/Farmington Hills.

The last glacier, known as the Wisconsin, left moraines or ridges in the Farmington area that extend as far south as Defiance, Ohio. The outer ridge of the Defiance Moraine can be seen at Twelve Mile Road as it rises toward Halsted Road, while the inner ridge is located just east of Drake Road, also along Twelve Mile Road. As a result, the highest elevation (over 900 feet above sea level) is in the northwest corner of Farmington Hills, while the lowest elevation (over 600 feet above sea level) is found in the southeast corner. The glacier's movement also altered the local terrain, covering this area with glacial till over 100 feet thick. The rich soil lay in silence only to be awakened years later by the men and women who settled here.

The first people to inhabit this area came from Siberia when the glacial period ended. Walking across the Bering Strait land bridge to Alaska, they settled throughout North America. Their descendants, the Potawatomi Indians, came from the northeast along with the Ottawa and Ojibwe. The three tribes united, calling themselves "The Three Fires." Eventually, the Ottawa settled around the islands of Lake Huron, while the Ojibwe and the Potawatomi continued on to Sault Ste. Marie.

The Potawatomi then migrated to Michigan's lower peninsula sometime during the 1400s. Some drifted southeast toward what is now Farmington/Farmington Hills, spreading across Lower Michigan's border and spilling into northern Illinois, Indiana, and northwestern Ohio. As such, they were one of Michigan's six major tribes (Chippewa, Fox, Miami, Ottawa, Sauk, and Potawatomi) who spoke an Algonquian dialect. *Potawatomi*, the name itself, means "the people of the place of fire" or "nation of fire." Covered with thick forests and rich with wildlife, the Farmington area was most likely one of their prized hunting grounds.

The Potawatomi lived in clans representing five social groups: the Leaders, the Warriors, the Healers, the Hunters, and the Teachers. Each Potawatomi Indian belonged to a specific clan determined by his or her ancestry. Clan members considered themselves brothers and sisters regardless of their parentage. Therefore, intermarrying within the clan was not allowed. A man seeking a wife had to choose a woman from a different clan. Eventually, as the population grew, so did the number of clans who still maintained a common language and who rarely fought among themselves. They were known to band together, however, when fighting occurred against other tribes such as the Iroquois or Sioux.

Their villages were seasonal and usually located along bodies of water much like Minnow Pond. In the summer, they lived in large, rectangular bark-covered houses that held up to five families. An opening was left along the top for light to come in and smoke to go out. Long benches, used as beds, were built along the walls of the structure. Personal items such as clothes and weapons hung from ceiling poles. In the fall, after buffalo hunting, they split up into smaller camps. In these camps, they built similar dome-shaped winter homes, but only big enough to hold four people. They slept on smaller benches, lined with sticks and brush and covered with animal furs.

Spiritual people, the Potawatomi believed in the gods of fire, sea, and sun, as well as the Great Spirit, Kitchemonedo, and the Evil Spirit, Matchemonedo. The Grand Medicine Society, their main religious group, healed the sick with medicines made from various roots and plants. Firm believers in the afterlife, they celebrated the departure of a deceased person's spirit, believing that the soul traveled over a trail, through the stars, and into heaven.

For the most part, the Potawatomi men hunted deer, elk, bear, rabbits, and beaver. These animals were sought not only for their meat, but for their pelts as well. The women farmed the land growing beans, peas, squash, melons, and corn. They also cultivated tobacco, considering it a gift from the gods. Both men and women fished in nearby lakes and streams. They gathered naturally grown foods such as blueberries for soup and nuts for roasting or pounding into flour. They also collected sap from the maple trees, which they made into syrup.

Early accounts describe the Michigan Potawatomi as short and dark skinned. In peaceful times, most warriors wore their hair long. In the summer, their simple clothes were made of red or blue cloth. During winter months, they donned intricately decorated buffalo robes and leggings. When preparing for battle, they shaved their heads except for a small scalp lock to which they fastened an eagle feather and a porcupine quill. The women wore long underskirts with knee-length dresses over them. Most covered their heads with bonnets or hoods attached to their robes. They wore a single long braid down their back. Men and women both greased their hair and painted themselves. Depending on the occasion, the men might use a variety of colors, while the women applied mainly red paint to their faces.

French fur traders were the first Europeans to claim Michigan for themselves. Needing help to trap furs, they befriended the local natives and put them to work. The first written account of the Potawatomi comes from Frenchman Jean Nicollet, the first white man to reach Michigan. Nicollet discovered a tribe of

This sketch depicts a Potawatomi Indian. His long hair indicates a time of peace. (Courtesy of the Farmington Community Library.)

Chief Pontiac led many Native Americans into battle against the British. The Ottawa leader was a staunch ally of the French. (Courtesy of the Walter P. Reuther Library, Wayne State University.)

Potawatomis living near Lake Huron in 1671. Thirty years later, Antoine de la Mothe Cadillac founded Detroit and settled on the banks of the Detroit River, leaving Michigan's interior to the Native Americans. Tolerant of the French who gave them firearms and employed them as fur trappers, the Potawatomi lived up to their reputation as a quiet, gentle, and hard-working people.

In 1707, an anonymous French colonist described the Potawatomi he knew:

> . . . the women do all the work [growing corn, beans, peas, squash and melons]. The men belonging to that nation are well clothed, like our domiciliated Indians at Montreal; their entire occupation is hunting and dress; they make use of a great deal of vermilion, and in winter wear buffalo robes richly painted and in summer either blue or red cloth. They play a good deal at la crosse in summer, twenty or more on each side. Their bat is a sort of little racket and the ball with which they play is made of very heavy wood, somewhat larger than the balls used at tennis; when playing they are entirely naked, except a breech cloth and moccasins on their feet. Their bodies are completely painted with all sorts of colors. Some, with white clay, trace white lace on their bodies, for silver lace. They play very deep and often. The bets sometimes amount to more than eight hundred livres. They set up two poles and

> commence the game from the center; one party propels the ball from one side and the other from the opposite, and whichever reaches the goal wins. This is fine recreation and worth seeing.

The Potawatomi were key allies to the French, even willing to fight alongside them against other tribes. They sided with the French when the Fox attacked Detroit's Fort Pontchartrain in 1712. Throughout the Fox Wars, which lasted until 1737, the Potawatomi remained staunch French supporters. Later on, during the French and Indian War, the Potawatomi fought with the French against the British, who were anxious to claim the Michigan territory for themselves. When the war ended in 1763, the British prevailed. With the French defeated, the Potawatomi were forced to trade with white men for whom they had no loyalty.

Under the leadership of the great Ottawa Chief Pontiac, many Native Americans, including the Potawatomi, attacked the British at Fort Detroit, hoping to put the French back in control. It was a bloody revolt, ending only when word reached Pontiac that the English and French had signed a peace treaty in Europe ceding the land east of the Mississippi to England. Good or bad, the Michigan territory was now in the hands of the British. In an attempt to keep peace with the Native Americans, the British developed the Proclamation of 1763 declaring that the natives could retain land west of the Appalachians, while the colonists would stay to the east. For the next several years, their plan worked despite the fact that white settlers slowly made their way west in direct opposition to the peace agreement.

By the time the American Revolution began in 1776, the Potawatomi and other Native Americans felt threatened by the settlers who were defiantly moving into their territory. In Michigan, the Detroit Potawatomi fought alongside the British when they raided American settlements in the midwest. They even brought American scalps to British governor Harry Hamilton, who gladly paid for each and every one. Even though the war ended with an American victory, local Native Americans, including the Potawatomi, united with the British, hoping to keep the white settlers out of what was now called the "Northwest Territory." Violent skirmishes ensued.

Finally, President George Washington sent one of his most experienced military men, General "Mad Anthony" Wayne, to stop the fighting. The Indians were stunned to learn that the British were forbidden by their homeland to fight with the Americans. Left to face their enemies alone, they wisely chose to make peace.

As a result, General Wayne negotiated the Treaty of Greenville in 1795. Michigan's four major Native American groups—the Wyandots, the Chippewas, the Ottawas, and the Potawatomi—participated. Chief New-corn, an old Potawatomi leader, asked his braves to give up their British medals. He requested that President Washington provide them with new ones and spoke eloquently on behalf of his people:

> . . . I come from Lake Michigan. Had you seen me in former days you would have beheld a great and brave chief, but now I am old and

> burdened with the weight of years. My nation consists of one thousand men who live at Detroit and between Detroit and Lake Michigan. Twenty-three chiefs of that nation are inferior to me in command. My young men will no longer listen to the former [the British]. They have thrown off the British and henceforth will view the Americans as their only friends.

Under the Treaty of Greenville, land in Ohio and Indiana was sold to the United States government. The Native Americans were allowed to maintain the rest of their land until the government decided to draw up another treaty and purchase it from them. Other than receiving a $1,000 signing bonus, the Potawatomi remained unaffected by this treaty. Their land, extending across Lower Michigan and into northern Ohio and Indiana, as well as Illinois and Wisconsin, was left untouched for the time being.

The United States government formally established and recognized the Michigan Territory in 1805. Despite this fact, the British remained in the area and continued doing business with the local Native Americans. It was almost as if nothing changed for the local Potawatomi. Two years later, President Thomas Jefferson decided to take over the eastern half of Michigan. As a result, the Treaty of Detroit was drawn up on November 17, 1807. For the first time, the Potawatomi gave up land that included what is now Oakland County where Farmington/Farmington Hills are located.

Many Native Americans were dissatisfied with this turn of events. Two Shawnee brothers, Chief Tecumseh and The Prophet Tenskwatawa, encouraged all Native Americans to unite against American expansion into their territory. The British encouraged the natives' revolt and, in 1811, the Battle of Tippecanoe (near what is now Lafayette, Indiana) ensued. There, the Native Americans' confederacy was busted, but it only served to deepen their hostility toward Americans and reaffirm their allegiance with the British.

As the unrest continued, the War of 1812 commenced and Michigan once again found itself under British rule. Their occupation was short-lived, however, as Commander Oliver Hazard Perry and the United States fleet defeated the British in the Battle of Lake Erie in September 1813. The British and their Native American allies headed toward Toronto. The Michigan Territory was returned to the United States government, putting an effective end to the Native Americans' revolt. The Detroit Potawatomi were only allowed to return to their land after signing the Treaty of Spring Wells in 1815 and agreeing to peace.

That same year, surveyors were sent into Michigan's interior where they found a "vast uncharted wilderness" in the Oakland County area. One of the surveyors, Captain Herve Parke, described what he saw: " . . . thick, dark forest, quaking marshland, buzzing mosquitoes, and packs of wolves."

The final report submitted to Washington in 1815 by Edward Tiffin, surveyor-general of this region, wasn't much kinder:

This image is a close-up of Farmington as it appeared on the 1825 map of the Michigan Territory. (Courtesy of the Farmington Community Library.)

> There would not be one acre out of a hundred, if there would be one out of a thousand that would, in any case, admit of cultivation . . . the intermediate space between the swamps and lakes, which is probably nearly one-half of the country, is, with very few exceptions, a poor barren, sandy land, on which scarcely any vegetation grows, except very small scrubby oaks.

Lewis Cass, the Michigan Territory's governor, refused to believe it. Anxious to meet population requirements and qualify for statehood, he knew it was imperative that settlers from the east be enticed to the area. Cass took matters into his own hands when he gathered a group of men and went to see for himself. Traveling northwest, the governor found that the marshland ended about 12 miles outside of Detroit, where, to his delight, he found "not a swamp, but rich land" fit for farming and a plentiful water supply. He didn't hesitate to spread the word. Thanks to Cass's persistence, the Michigan Territory was now an appealing place for settlers to come.

Based on the customary latitude and longitude lines, townships were divided into 36-square-mile sections containing a total of 640 acres each. By 1817, the first official map of the Farmington area was certified and published by the surveyor-general.

Although this formal map detailed only one Indian trail, the Shiawassee, there were actually three main trails that crossed through Farmington/Farmington Hills. The Orchard Lake Trail broke off from the Old Sauk Trail in the city of Wayne. It traveled north along present-day Farmington Road, crossed the Grand River Trail at what is now Freedom Road, and then crossed the Shiawassee Trail near the site of the First Baptist Church of Farmington, continuing north until it reached Orchard Lake.

The Grand River Trail originated in the Dearborn area where it traveled along Freedom Road, crossing Farmington Road, and on to Gill Road where it made a northwest turn toward Drake Road and eventually reached the Grand River on the far west side of the territory. The Shiawassee Trail originated from the Saginaw Trail, located in what is now the city of Highland Park. This trail crossed today's Eight Mile Road, traveled through Farmington/Farmington Hills along what is now Shiawassee Road, where it continued in a northwest direction leading to the central area of the state. The three main roads in Farmington/Farmington Hills today follow these same trails.

By 1820, the Potawatomi Indians were forced to give up the majority of their Michigan land to the United States government. In turn, the government sold the land to settlers interested in moving west for $1.25 an acre. The land west of Detroit where the three main Indian trails met was particularly tempting. And so it was, in 1824, that Arthur Power, a Quaker from Farmington, New York came to Michigan and the Potawatomi Curtain fell for the final time.

This photograph shows the Rouge River the way the Potawatomi must have viewed it. (Photo by Tim Ostrander.)

2. QUAKERTOWN

Arthur Power was born on November 14, 1771 in Providence, Rhode Island. His parents and two older brothers came to the British colonies from England. During the Revolutionary War, his brothers joined Washington's army and were lost in battle. After his father's death, Power and his mother moved to South Adams, Massachusetts. Restless, Power eventually struck out on his own. He went to New York where he purchased land with the $100 his mother had given him. There he married a Massachusetts native, Deborah Aldrich. After giving birth to seven sons (John, Ira, Nathan, Jared, Samuel, Abram, and William) and four daughters (Duana, Mary, Bulah, and Esther), she died in 1817.

Arthur Power remarried. His second wife Mary Dillingham presented him with two girls, Deborah (named for the first Mrs. Power) and Duana (probably named for Power's first-born daughter, who most likely died). Shortly after the birth of her second daughter, Mary Dillingham Power died in 1823. That's when twice-widowed Arthur Power made his momentous decision.

Like many settlers from the east, Power wanted more. He looked west with the hopes of giving himself and his family a secure future. A Quaker from Farmington, New York, Power first came to Michigan in 1823 simply to check the place out. He camped along what is now Orchard Lake and Ten Mile Roads beside a spring. Intrigued by the Michigan wilderness, Power entered a claim in Oakland County, purchasing 2,000 acres of land in Sections 22, 27, and 28. A man of vision and imagination, he saw potential in the heavily wooded area we now know as Farmington and Farmington Hills. Instead of insurmountable forests, he saw plentiful timber. He viewed the nearby river as a main source of power where mills might flourish, and the sandy soil as a means to support thriving farms. No doubt a man of considerable foresight, he glimpsed the future.

Power permanently left his Ontario County home in western New York in early February 1824, while James Monroe was still president. A man with a purpose, he once again headed for the untamed lands of the Michigan Territory. Accompanying him on his great adventure were two of his sons, John and Jared, along with hired hands David Smith and Daniel Rush. The younger children were left behind in the care of their older brother Nathan and sister Mary.

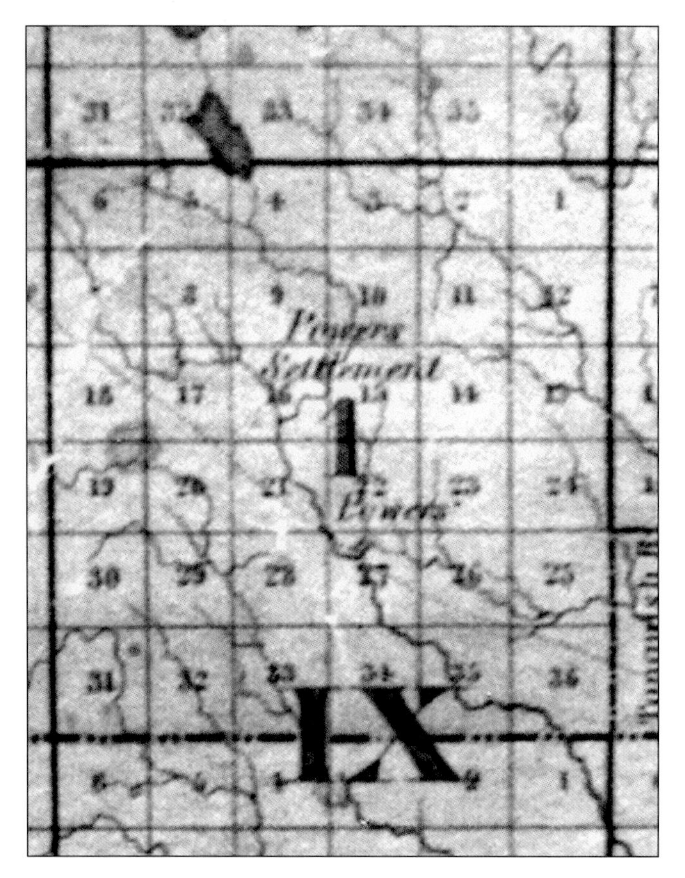

This is an 1825 map of Power Settlement. Note the gridlines dividing the area into square-mile sections. (Courtesy of the Farmington Community Library.)

Their journey took over a month as the small group traveled through Canada by horse-drawn sleigh, crossing the Niagara River and arriving at Windsor on February 15. They rode over the frozen Detroit River and stopped in the city of Detroit where they purchased supplies before continuing along the Saginaw Trail (now Woodward Avenue) to their final destination. The group arrived at their new residence, a heavily wooded area near today's intersection of Eleven Mile and Power Roads, on March 8. Power and company promptly christened it Farmington after its New York counterpart. It must have made them feel more at home.

A daunting task lay before them, but they tackled it with the same gumption that it took to leave New York. Not ones to waste time, they went right to work that very same day chopping down the first tree to make way for their new home. By spring, they built a log house and cleared 15 acres of land—9 for wheat and 6 for corn. Power promised that first house to his son Nathan, so later that summer, he built a second home about 1 mile further south directly on the Shiawassee Trail near the banks of the Upper Rouge River. An ambitious man, he purchased 160 acres for each of his sons. Mary and Nathan, however, each earned an extra 80 acres for staying behind in New York. It was their father's way of thanking them for looking after the younger children and minding the family farm in his absence.

While Power and his sons settled in, Daniel Rush grew homesick. After only three weeks, he left the settlement on foot heading for Detroit with every intention of going home. David Smith, however, remained in Power's service for the next year. Earning himself $136, Smith then purchased land where, according to the Oakland County History written in 1877, he remained well into his 80s.

Several weeks after the Powers' arrival, New Yorkers George Collins and his pregnant wife Cynthia joined them, giving Cynthia Collins the distinction of being the first white woman to settle in Farmington. While George tended to the business of building a house, Cynthia saw to it that the men were well fed. The township's third resident, Wardwell Green, came from Orleans County, New York where he was born in 1793. One of 13 children, Green, a staunch Whig supporter, settled here in May 1824 where he became a well-respected member of the community with a reputation for honesty and strict morality.

As summer turned into fall, the township experienced other firsts. Cynthia Collins delivered the first white child, born in Farmington on September 26, 1824. They named him John. Ironically, on that very same day of celebration, the township also suffered its first death and burial. Two months earlier, 52-year-old Patience Utley took a nasty fall from the family wagon just as the Utleys approached the township sighting their land in the English settlement for the very first time.

This is the old Eagle Mill on Power Road north of Grand River in 1905. John Power is the tallest man standing on the porch. (Courtesy of the Farmington Community Library.)

East Farmington Cemetery is on Twelve Mile Road. The land was originally part of the Utley farm. (Photo by Tim Ostrander.)

When she finally succumbed to her injuries, her husband Sanford buried her on the farm owned by their son Peleg. Four years later, their 18-year-old son Samuel also died and was buried near his mother. This section of the Utley Farm became Farmington's first cemetery, known as the Utley Cemetery. Located on today's Twelve Mile between Inkster and Middlebelt Roads, the cemetery has since been renamed East Farmington Cemetery.

Later, in 1824, Dr. Ezekiel Webb and his wife Fanny, fellow-Quakers as well as friends and neighbors of Arthur Power back in New York, also settled here. With their help, Power established a frontier community that could now boast the services of a capable physician. It was a triumphant moment for the fragile little town that seemed to be taking root.

When the Erie Canal opened in 1825, travel to the Michigan territory was even easier, beckoning more New England settlers. Other families like the Thayers, Wixoms, and Warners also arrived and built homes in the community. Many of these pioneers were also hardworking Quakers with high moral standards and religious principles. As a result (and much to Arthur Power's irritation), Farmington, now considered Michigan's first Quaker settlement, became known as Quakertown.

Like Arthur Power, Rufus Thayer Jr. came to Michigan from New York in 1823 and bought land. The deed to his property near Halsted and Nine Mile is dated September 29, 1823. Thayer also returned home where he worked for the next two years preparing for life in the western territory. He came back to Michigan accompanied by his brothers in 1825. The next year, their father Rufus Sr. followed. Born in Massachusetts in 1767, he was the fifth generation of the Thayer family to be born in America. The senior Thayer brought along his wife and four daughters. Young, single women on the frontier were a rare sight and the presence of the Thayer sisters in Farmington was a welcome one.

The Wixoms were another early pioneer family who bought land in Michigan in 1823. Robert Wixom Sr. had nine children—five sons and four daughters. Benjamin, his second son, was the first to arrive here. He purchased land for his family in Section 15 (Twelve Mile and Farmington Road where the Orchard Ridge Campus of Oakland County Community College now stands). His eldest son Ahijah moved further west where he founded the city of Wixom. Isaac, his third son, was a doctor, but didn't arrive in Farmington until 1830. His fourth son and namesake, Robert Wixom Jr., was one of the original founders of the Village of Farmington. Civilian, the youngest son, ran one of Farmington's first taverns. Sally, Wixom's eldest daughter, married Seth Andrew LeMoyne Warner, who also hailed from New York. In 1825, the Warners also left their home back east and soon joined the Wixoms in Farmington.

Seth and Sally Warner traveled by steamboat to Detroit, taking an overland trail through Dearborn, and then on to Farmington where Sally was reunited with her family. With them were their three sons, William Smith Warner, Robert Wixom Warner, and their youngest child, two-year-old Pascal D'Angelis Warner. His unusual name came from a sea captain who was the first husband of Seth Warner's mother—a man she married in the West Indies. Originally from England, the Warner family came to America in 1626, settling first in Massachusetts and then Connecticut. After the Revolutionary War and the War of 1812, the family moved to Hector, New York where Pascal was born in 1822. Migrating further west seemed the natural thing to do.

Pascal, who later called himself P. Dean, recollected those early years in Farmington when he addressed the County Pioneer Society in 1879:

> Nearly twenty families had settled in the town during the year previous to our coming—Arthur Power having been the first actual resident, coming March 8, 1824, and others coming in about the following order: George W. Collins, Benjamen Wixom, Timothy Tolman, Judah Marsh, Sanford Utley, Solomon Woodfrod, Robert Wixom, Edward Steele, Howland Mason, Hiram Wilmarth, Wardwell Green, Leland Green, Solomon Walker, Hezekiah Smith, George Brownell, and Matthew Van Amburg. In 1825 about the same number of families were added to the population of the settlement, and among them were those of Samuel Mead, Amos Mead, Philip Marlet, Elisha Cooley, Elisha Doty, Jonathan Lewis, Thomas Jophns, Absalom Barnum, Constantine Wood, and my father. From this time Farmington began to have quite a reputation as being a favorable locality in which to make a desirable settlement and

> large numbers availed themselves of the opportunity of buying and occupying farms in Farmington . . .

Settling in the northwest corner of Section 15 (now Twelve Mile and Farmington Roads), Seth Warner opened a merchandising business and was one of only six Oakland County residents elected to represent the Michigan Territory. It was at the First Convention of Assent in 1836 when the first proposal of statehood was declined. The representatives turned down statehood, preferring to include the Toledo, Ohio area instead of the Upper Peninsula. One year later, during the second convention, Michigan entered the Union, but once again without the approval of Oakland County's representatives.

As the opening of the new Erie Canal profoundly affected westward travel, Arthur Power profoundly affected Farmington. He understood the importance of community. Individual farmers heading west could not survive alone. It would be impossible. People needed businesses and industry, no matter how small, to ensure their future and reinforce their sense of community.

With that in mind, Power started a potash works in 1825. Using the Upper Rouge River as a source of power, he built a sawmill in 1826, followed by a gristmill along the Shiawassee Trail two years later. Just as the potash works provided soap, one of life's necessities, the sawmill enabled the settlers to upgrade from their log homes to frame ones, while the gristmills ground their grain into flour with relative ease. Regardless of their size, Power's enterprises served to establish a burgeoning business center for the nearby residents who farmed the land. As luck, or fate, would have it, Power chose a strategic spot on the Shiawassee Trail, which was wide enough to hold a horse and wagon. The trail soon turned into the Detroit Road, connecting the tiny town with the larger city—Detroit.

The year 1826 was memorable for Arthur Power for personal reasons as well. In addition to his sawmill, he built his third and final home. He was also reunited with his 25-year-old son Nathan, who came from New York to join his father in the Michigan Territory. In his diary, Nathan Power described his journey:

> We started from Father Payne's [Power's father-in-law] the fifth day of the week, first of sixth month, 1826. Arrived at Buffalo first day, morning, fourth of sixth month. Stayed in Buffalo two days waiting for boat. Left there on the "Henry Clay" for Detroit. Arrived there . . . being one night and about two days on the lake. In two days after we arrived at Father's house on the north bank of the mill stream tenth of sixth month, 5 o'clock p.m.
>
> . . . twenty days after we had arrived I got our stove and furniture from Detroit so that we began to keep house in the first one built in the town. Our journey from Father Payne's to Michigan was just ten days. Gideon [Nathan Power's firstborn] was six and a half months old.

Nathan Power was Farmington's first official schoolteacher. (Courtesy of the Farmington Community Library.)

Although he may not have known it at the time, Nathan Power was destined to become a major presence in Farmington. His influence would be felt for years. Upon his arrival, he began teaching in Farmington's first school—a small log building near the creek. As the community grew, the need for a new schoolhouse became apparent. In 1835, Power was granted the handsome sum of $375 for the building of a new school. The two-story structure, also made of logs, was erected near McGee Hill just above the Upper Rouge River. Known throughout the district as "The Little Red Schoolhouse," it remained in use until 1852, when Power built an even larger school.

A resourceful man, Power not only taught school and farmed, he also hunted wolves in his spare time for extra money. Back then, the state offered an $8 bounty, while the county paid $5, for every wolf caught. With an abundance of wolves in the area, it turned into a lucrative business that nicely supplemented a teacher's salary and helped tremendously with purchases for the farm.

Another important event occurred in 1826 when the community rallied together to build the Webbs a new home in Section 28. The large double-log home, built on Division Street (now Farmington Road) just south of the Shiawassee Trail, is the only home left from that era and is still in use as a private residence. The house itself also served as Farmington's first post office. Mail came weekly from Detroit and was delivered by Dr. Webb, known to carry letters in his hat while making house calls to the 20 or so families who lived here.

In the spring of 1827, several new townships were recognized in the Michigan Territory—among them Farmington. Normally, the territory's governor appointed township officials, but Michigan's governor, Lewis Cass, was different. He believed that local residents should have the right to elect their own officials. Therefore, he urged Congress to pass an act allowing citizens of a township to elect their own officers. With the exception of judges, clerks, and sheriffs, Congress complied. Still not satisfied, however, Cass urged people of the new townships to vote for the men of their choice in even these positions. He would in turn make his appointments accordingly. Farmington then became one of the first townships to choose all of its own officials by ballot. Casting their votes, the people selected Amos Mead as the first township supervisor.

Amos Mead had also come to Farmington from New York. The son of "Fat Timothy" Mead, an innkeeper, he not only helped organize the fledgling township, but the first Presbyterian Church as well. Opening his home to services, in 1826, he welcomed Pontiac's Reverend Isaac W. Ruggles to preach until a more permanent arrangement could be made. In addition, Mead's daughter Polly Ann was Farmington's first female teacher, taking over for Nathan Power during the summer term so he could work his farm.

With Amos Mead in charge, the township held its first meeting at the home of Robert Wixom Jr. on May 28, 1827. The business at hand was as follows:

The Old Wixom Inn Tavern on Grand River near Ten Mile was known for its lively parties. (Courtesy of the Farmington Community Library.)

> Article 1, a fence of strong and sound materials of five feet in height and so close that hogs and sheep cannot creep through, or a hedge two feet high upon a ditch three feet deep and three feet broad, or instead of such hedge, a fence three feet high, the hedge or fence being so done that the animals aforesaid cannot creep through. Shall be accounted a Lawful fence—Provided however that no person shall be obliged to fence pigs weighing less than thirty pounds.
>
> Article 2, all stallions of the age of twenty months and over shall be restrained from going at large on the public highway or Commons within said Township under the penalty of the sum of ten dollars to be recovered with costs of suite by the Supervisor of the said Township.

It was a farming community, after all.

Later that same year, Solomon Walker opened Farmington's first tavern, located on present-day Grand River and Halsted. Originally called the Walker Inn, the log building itself was plain and simple, but as owner and host, Walker knew how to throw a party. He organized a huge New Year's Eve celebration to ring in 1828. That night, the Walker Inn overflowed with guests—mainly younger people willing to travel over rough roads with their oxen and horses in the dead of winter just to have a good time. The inn soon became known for its social gatherings and eventually township meetings were held there. Walker built a second tavern just east of his original inn. He later sold the Walker Inn to Nathan S. Philbrick, who in turn sold it to Robert Wixom Jr. Renamed the Wixom Inn, the tavern prospered and an addition was put on as it became a stopping point for Detroit's Hibbard and Burrill Stage Coach Line.

Nathan S. Philbrick and his wife Minerva traveled to Farmington in the spring of 1825 from Niagara County, New York. They purchased 160 acres in Section 15 for the going rate of $1.25 each. The Orchard Lake Indian Trail cut right across their land as it traveled to Pontiac, the county seat. After selling the Walker Inn, the couple went on to build the Philbrick Tavern in 1828. Well known for its oversized second-floor ballroom, the inn's high standards of service enhanced its popularity. Centrally located, township meetings were also held at the Philbrick Tavern. As well as being an innkeeper, Philbrick himself served as justice of the peace in 1834, 1838, and 1840. His large, white tavern, now a private residence, is still located on Eleven Mile and Power Roads.

As more settlers called Farmington home, the little frontier town flourished. By 1830, Arthur Power married for the third time. He and his new wife Sarah Lawton continued living in Farmington raising the three youngest Power children. Stephen Page opened Farmington's first store at the intersection of Division Road and Shiawassee Trail, by now the center of town. Arthur Power built another general store for Henry Miller and a shoemaker shop for his son-in-law Ebenezer Stevens, now Mary's husband. The Dutcher Brothers opened a blacksmith shop, while George Collins followed with his own store in 1831. It was a large red building on the corner of Division Road and Grand River—later used as a meeting place for the Universalist Church. With the exception of George Collins's store, most of these fledgling businesses were run right inside the entrepreneurs' homes, the front part reserved for conducting business while the back part, or in some cases the second floor, served as living quarters.

Farmington's sense of community was also enhanced by its military. Organized in 1831 and led by Captain Warren Lee, along with First Lieutenant George Brown and Orderly Sergeant Fitz Smith, the finely trained militia was a credit to the township. Proud of their very own sharpshooters, known as the "Farmington Riflemen," the soldiers were often referred to as "minute-men." The corps could be called upon in a moment's notice to defend the frontier. Wearing gray uniforms and donning green-feathered hats, they trained vigorously in Walled Lake, along with other local soldiers. The troop remained in existence until after the Civil War.

As community ties strengthened, Arthur Power and Dr. Webb experienced some sort of falling out. The actual cause, believed to be a property dispute, was left unrecorded. As a result, in 1830, the good doctor and his wife sold their home on Division Street to George Collins and moved further west to Lansing. Collins most likely wanted the house because of its close proximity to his store. Nonetheless, when he moved in, Collins not only established a small potash factory, but also took over the doctor's official duties as postmaster. In addition to his work as township treasurer, Collins served as postmaster for the next 25 years. When he died in 1865, his wife Cynthia remained in the house on Division Street until her own death at the age of 93. With Dr. Webb's absence, however, the town not only needed a postmaster, but a physician as well. Isaac Wixom filled the bill nicely, taking over the doctor's duties tending to the medical needs of the township's residents.

Throughout those first years, the Quakers sporadically gathered together for services. There were no formal meetings, nor was there an official meeting place. The Quakers in Michigan, however, did remain in close contact with their fellow Quakers back east. Concerned about the settlers' lack of structure, nine delegates from New York visited Farmington in 1831, establishing a formal Quaker society with quarterly meetings. Arthur Power donated land for the meetinghouse.

Built in 1832, the traditional white-frame meetinghouse, with its oblong shape, was similar to those back east. Outdoors, a long porch ran along one side. Indoors, the hall was divided into two large rooms—one for the women and one for the men. Separated by shutters, the two groups conducted their own affairs of business. They only came together for services, at which time the shutters were opened. In addition to the simple benches the congregation used, there was a three-tiered gallery of benches stationed along the wall opposite the entrance. These seats, appropriately called "facing benches," were reserved for the ministers and elders who sat facing the rest of the group. Members dressed very simply for their First-Day meetings, which were held every Sunday. The men wore collarless coats with broad-brimmed hats, and the women wore plain gray or purple dresses with linen caps or bonnets. The frequency and consistency of these meetings served to strengthen the community's bonds.

The land adjoining the meetinghouse was reserved for a cemetery. Located on what is now Gill Road, the cemetery is believed to be the oldest Quaker landmark in Michigan. Ironically, Nathan Power's wife and daughter were the first to be buried in the new graveyard, victims of the cholera epidemic that ravaged the frontier.

Within a year after the meetinghouse was built and the cemetery established, cholera came to Farmington via the *Henry Clay*—the very same steamer that originally carried Nathan Power and his family from Buffalo. The *Henry Clay* docked in Detroit on July 4, 1832. On board were more than 300 soldiers heading west for the Black Hawk War. Several soldiers, stricken with an unknown disease, disembarked. One died the very next day.

Soon, hundreds of Detroiters fell ill with what doctors diagnosed as Asiatic Cholera. Ultimately, 100 residents succumbed to the disease. The most famous was the indomitable Father Gabriel Richard, who not only co-founded the University of Michigan, but played a significant role in shaping the city of Detroit. It is believed that Farmington resident Absalom Barnum was visiting Detroit when the *Henry Clay* arrived. Upon returning home, a grave illness overtook him and he died. Nathan Power was among the men who buried him.

Two weeks later, Power's wife Selinda became violently ill with severe stomach pains. Her condition worsened and Dr. Wixom was summoned. Recognizing cholera, there was little he could do for the dying woman. By early the next

The Quakertown Cemetery on Gill Road is believed to be the oldest Quaker landmark in Michigan. (Photo by Tim Ostrander.)

Land for Oakwood Cemetery on Grand River was donated by Arthur Power. (Photo by Tim Ostrander.)

morning, Selinda was gone. Their young daughter Phebe Minerva was also found ill and she too died that same day. Mother and daughter were buried together on August 7, 1832 in the new Quaker cemetery. Four months later on Christmas Eve, Nathan's 13-month-old son George also died of unrelated causes and was buried with his mother and sister.

As 1832 drew to a close, a disheartened Nathan Power described the unimaginable events:

> Selinda Payne my first wife died of the Asiatic Cholera being thirty-two years old. My only daughter, Phebe Minerva, five years old, died the same day at eleven o'clock and Selinda at seven a.m. They were buried in our ground the same day at six o'clock. The first grave opened in our cemetery . . . and my little George who was the last gift of his mother . . . make just half of my family that I have this year followed to the silent grave.
>
> This is a year long to be remembered by me; a year never to be forgotten while in mutability it has been a dispensation of deep trial that none knows save those that are called upon to pass through.

Two years later, Power married Patience Comstock, who bore him two more children. Despite a good, long life with her, Power never forgot his personal tragedy. Seventeen years after losing his loved ones, he still mourned:

> . . . after meeting, I borrowed a spade and raised the earth over the grave of my dear departed wife and daughter, Minerva. This was a piece of work that I had promised myself that I would do for many years.

As difficult as 1832 proved to be, it also brought with it a stroke of good luck for the people of Farmington. The War of 1812 had made it obvious that better roads were needed if men and supplies were to be easily transported through the country's interior. Therefore, Congress approved funds for the building of military roads. Money was appropriated for the construction of one such road along the Grand River Trail.

At the time, travel to and from Detroit was anything but easy. Even though the Grand River Trail led directly to Detroit, it passed through swamps and marshes, making it difficult to cross. A second route to Detroit followed the Shiawassee Trail, snaking along the banks of the Rouge River ultimately leading to the Detroit River. The Native Americans themselves used this trail twice a year as they traveled from their reservation just outside Lansing to collect their government bounty in Detroit.

The settlers, however, preferred a third route along the Orchard Lake Trail. It led to Pontiac where it met Saginaw Road, which then traveled on to Detroit. At a distance of 38 miles, it was definitely the lengthiest route of the three, but it was the easiest to cross and kept travel time to Detroit down to two days.

Construction of the Grand River Territorial Road started in 1833. Within four years, it passed right through Farmington, extending as far west as Howell. Now, the distance between Farmington and Detroit was a mere 20 miles, which cut travel time in half and attracted even more settlers to the area.

Shortly before the road was finished, Farmington's founder, 64-year-old Arthur Power, died on August 6, 1836 from consumption—an old-fashioned word for tuberculosis. He was buried in the Quaker Cemetery. A saddened Nathan described his father's death:

> This day I have completed my thirty-sixth year and with it had gone my beloved father who wasted away with the consumption. Though slow in its progress yet sure in its grasp on man and shows the mortality of our species. He was resigned to his lot and his death was calm and peaceful.

Power's widow Sarah married Charles Haviland and eventually moved to Ohio. Nonetheless, Arthur Power left behind a well-established community to continue what he started. Now, with Farmington's fortunate position directly on the new road, the township's growth was assured. The first stage line, which ran from Detroit to Howell, passed through the area in 1837, and with it a new chapter in Farmington's history was about to begin.

The summer of 1837 also welcomed Sergius P. Lyon and his wife Lucinda Davis, another pair of New Yorkers. A handyman, Lyon was sought for his building skills and was often called upon to help with raising barns and houses in the area. In 1844, he moved to the Village of Farmington where he opened his own business—manufacturing self-regulating stoves made by hand from sheet iron. After 13 years of stove making, he started the community's first undertaking business, building a set of his own first-rate hearses—one of which remained in use well into the 1920s.

In addition to his handiwork, Lyon also brought the Universalist Church to Farmington. He sought out Reverend E.M. Wooley, a traveling preacher from Pontiac, and talked him into holding services in Farmington. At first, they used a room above a wagon shop before moving to George Collins's store where they not only held services but established a Christian school. From there, Lyon founded the "Union Church" and encouraged people of all faiths and denominations to attend. He asked only that they believe in the teachings of Jesus. Before long, so many locals attended the services that the floor had to be reinforced and, in 1852, the Universalists built their own church at a cost of $900.

With the establishment of churches and schools and the arrival of more settlers from the east, traffic increased and so did local trade. The first *Michigan Gazeteer* described the area in 1838:

The Union/Universalist Church (c. 1900) was built in 1853 for $900 by Sergius P. Lyon. (Courtesy of the Farmington Community Library.)

This sketch shows Sergius P. Lyons's residence from the Oakland County History of 1877. (Courtesy of the Farmington Community Library.)

> Farmington contains two flouring mills with three run of stone—one propelled by water and the other by steam—two sawmills, two stores, one druggist, two physicians, and perhaps, twenty families. This is a flourishing community and it is surrounded by fine farming country.

The settlers, threatened by illness, hardship, and their own isolation, worked hard to survive. Forced to deal with the elements, there were dry, hot summers when they faced draughts and long, cold winters when they endured sub-freezing temperatures. The winter of 1843 to 1844, often called the "hard winter," went down in history as one of the worst. The prior June, there was a killing frost with ice so thick it could be scooped up by the handful. Crops were lost and, with no hay or grain, there was little to feed the livestock. Later in the year, as heavy snowfall after snowfall covered the ground, cattle and horses starved or froze to death. The following April, 2 feet of snow remained on the ground. By May 1, Detroiters were still walking across the frozen Detroit River.

Nathan Power made the following entry in his diary:

> This is set down as the coldest and most snowy and longest winter that has been in 50 years. The first thawing day was on the first day of [the] fourth month, and there was as much snow on the ground on that day as perhaps had fallen in the five preceeding winters. My pump had frozen every night so as to be thawed with a hot shovel handle until the

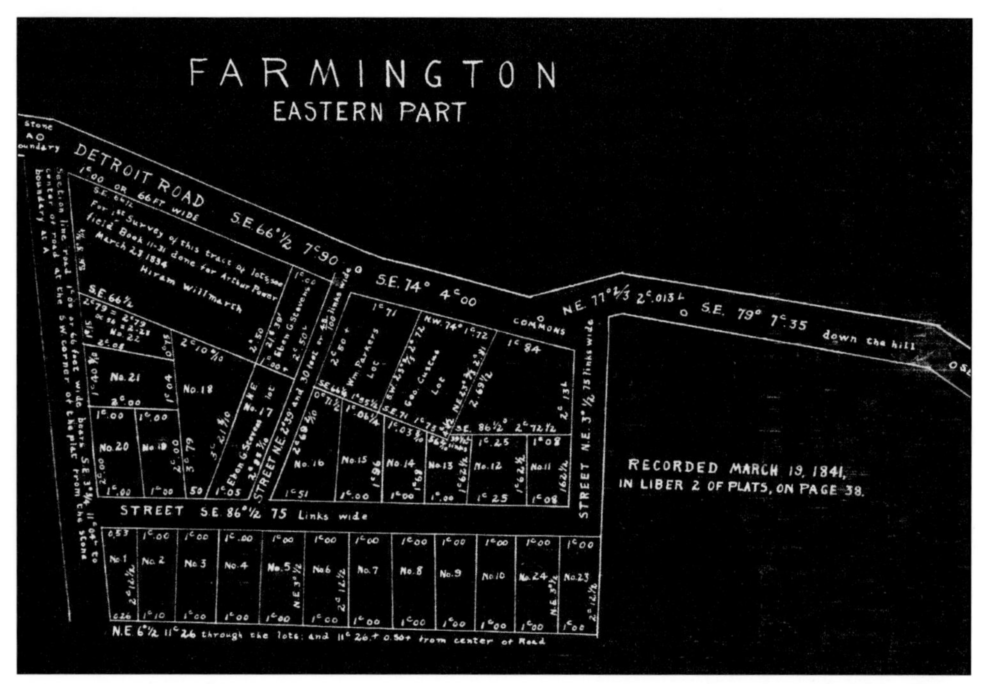

This map shows the eastern part of Farmington, c. 1850. (Courtesy of the Farmington Community Library.)

> morning of the third [day] of the fourth month. It continued so cold that I did not tap trees until the sixth of [the] fourth month. This was the extreme cold winter in which so many cattle and other stock died, perhaps one-fourth of the whole in the state died during the winter and spring. I lost seven calves . . . and three cows and three sheep. . . . This is the winter never to be forgotten, the gloomy dreary winter.

That same winter also brought with it Halley's comet. Many believed it to be a bad omen. A man from New York visited Farmington that year and proclaimed that he had had a vision of the earth and the comet colliding, thus causing the end of the world. He even displayed pictures of the disaster, while warning people to repent because the end was at hand. The end didn't come, however. Instead, the comet disappeared and spring finally turned into a much-welcomed summer.

By 1850, the main business district of Farmington was firmly ensconced at the intersection of Division Road and Shiawassee Trail, but once again, fate stepped in. A fire swept through the downtown area, destroying many of the businesses located there. The *Detroit Free Press* reported the following in March 1850:

> A fire broke out in the public house kept by Horace Swan, and before any assistance could be obtained, the flames had spread with such rapidity that it was impossible to arrest their progress until the entire

> building had melted before their fury. After which it communicated with the dwelling house owned and occupied by Civilian Wixom, which was also totally destroyed together with a small building, which was used for the storage of provender, etc. Mr. Swan's loss was only his building—he having had time to remove its contents. Estimated loss $2,000, with no insurance.

The decision was made not only to rebuild, but also to move the downtown area directly to Grand River, thereby accommodating the increased number of stagecoach travelers passing through the area.

Horace Swan was just one of the businessmen forced to reestablish his interests. He ran a successful tavern near the creek before the fire consumed it. The following year, he constructed a fine establishment on the corner of Grand River Trail and Division Road. The Swan, renamed the Farmington Hotel (later called the Owen House), became an important stop for stagecoaches on their way to and from Lansing. Twice a day, four horses pulling a stagecoach drove right through the center of town, announcing its arrival with a blast of a tin horn. Each stagecoach carried 24 travelers and often had up to nine additional passengers riding on top.

From its inception as a small town in 1824, Farmington grew into a bustling community supplying the surrounding farmers with various services, household goods, and farming equipment. With the building of the new road and the increase in traffic, Farmington also became a way station for travelers, as well as a service point for the many stages and wagons that passed through every day as they traveled between Detroit and Lansing.

The Quakers, however, failed to flourish along with the city. The older ones died, while the younger ones joined other religious groups. Nathan Power wrote the following in his diary in 1854:

> Our meetings are small this year. The Moores had moved away last year to Ypsilanti . . . Mother Payne and Reuben Payne have died last month. The ranks of our friends and relatives are thinning.

With so few members remaining, the weekly meetings were eventually discontinued and the local Society of Friends disbanded. Nathan Power moved into the meetinghouse and made it his home. Despite the fact that the religious affiliations of Arthur Power disappeared, the city he founded prospered. There is no doubt that Arthur Power knew a good thing when he saw it.

3. Other Local Settlements

While Arthur Power and his fellow Quakers were busy establishing the center of town, several other settlements sprung up throughout the area. Ideal for supporting various mills, the Upper Rouge River attracted many venturesome spirits as it cut its course across the untamed land. Sleepy Hollow, or Pernambuco Hollow as it was later called, was situated near Drake and Howard Roads. The English Settlement, so named for its many British residents, was bounded between Thirteen and Fourteen Mile Roads along Middlebelt and Inkster. A third settlement known as Clarenceville was set up directly on the Grand River Trail in the extreme southeastern corner of Farmington township near today's Eight Mile Road. North Farmington, another major settlement, developed at the intersection of Fourteen Mile and Farmington Roads and extended 1 mile south. In conjunction with the main business district located in the heart of Quakertown, these tiny communities, unique in their own right, intertwined, thus ensuring not only their success, but their ability to survive.

Sleepy Hollow

Like Arthur Power, the Steele brothers, Edward and Harmon, also came from New York in 1824. They bought 240 acres of land on the southeastern corner of Section 17 in what was to become the tiny settlement of Sleepy Hollow. Then they returned home. Three years later, the brothers, along with Edward's wife Louisa Murray, traveled back to Michigan. This time, they were well prepared to farm and build a gristmill along the fast-moving waters that rushed across their property. In 1827, the brothers opened the Steele Gristmill, located about 2.5 miles northwest of Quakertown. They hired millwright and machinist Howland Mason to run it. The following year, Louisa had a son, Carlos—the second white baby born in Farmington.

Local farmer Orange Culver, of English descent, was the Steele Gristmill's very first customer. His father George was a member of the Whig political party and a captain in the War of 1812. A Republican, Culver came to Farmington from New York in 1825. He bought undeveloped land in Section 10 where he built a log cabin. His nearest neighbors lived in Pontiac. Culver walked to the mill from his farm at today's Twelve Mile and Farmington Roads, hauling a sack of grain on his shoulders only to return home carrying a sack of flour.

The gristmill was the first of its kind in Oakland County. A rousing success, it drew not only local farmers, but those from neighboring Wayne County as well. Four years later, the brothers made Mason, who also owned 160 acres at the Grand River and Halsted intersection, a partner. Soon, a town known as Sleepy Hollow sprouted up around the gristmill and several businesses appeared. Among them were a slaughterhouse and tannery run by James Boorn, who also owned a shoemaker's shop, apparently by design. Boorn, a clever man, was known to make shoes right from the very hides he tanned. Eventually, two sawmills were also built in Sleepy Hollow—one by an enterprising Edward Steele and the other by a man of the cloth, Erie Prince.

Sent here by the American Home Missionary Society, the Reverend Erie Prince came to Farmington with his wife Caroline. He became the official minister of the Farmington Presbyterian Church following the Reverend Ruggles's sporadic appearances. The couple built a home along Howard Road and, since missionary work alone did not provide enough income to live on, they opened the Prince Sawmill along the Upper Rouge River in 1835. An official Presbyterian Church was finally built at Eleven Mile and Halsted in 1833, but several years later, it was relocated to Farmington's main business district near Shiawassee. In the meantime, Prince founded another church in Novi and, for a time, served both congregations with the two churches splitting his salary. Prince, a civic-minded

The Sleepy Hollow Miller's Cottage is on Drake and Howard Roads. (Photo by Tim Ostrander.)

individual, also held the position of Farmington Township supervisor from 1842 to 1844.

As the Presbyterian church took shape, so did the First Baptist Church. Farmington's First Baptist Church originated in 1826 at a council meeting held in Robert Wixom's home. If members wanted to attend more formal services, they had no choice but to travel to Pontiac. The journey proved difficult, so Elkanah Comstock, Michigan's first Baptist pastor, came to Farmington in 1826 and organized a local church. During the winter season, he held services in the West Farmington School, then in a log building at Halsted and Twelve Mile Roads built in 1826. In the summer, services moved to Samuel Mead's (brother of Amos) barn. Things changed, however, when the Reverend Nehemiah Lamb took over in 1833.

Sent to Farmington by the Baptist Home Missionary Society, Lamb was a traveling missionary with two sons who were also missionaries—Caleb, a homeopathic physician, and Aroswell, married to Robert Wixom Sr.'s second daughter Phebe. Like most ministers of the time, Lamb played a dual role in the community. In addition to his church duties, he farmed. He also made sure that his church members had their own meeting place. In 1835, under Reverend Lamb's direction, the First Baptist Church was built at Twelve Mile and Halsted Roads—1 mile north of the Presbyterian Church. Lamb also established the West Farmington Cemetery, located on the church grounds, and served at the

This historical marker is in front of the First Baptist Church of Farmington and Shiawasee Roads. (Photo by Tim Ostrander.)

new church until 1837 when he moved on to establish Baptist churches in both Livingston and Washtenaw Counties. Eventually, Farmington's First Baptist Church also moved to the main business district in 1857 on Shiawassee Trail where it stands today.

Caleb recalled those early years:

> In the spring of 1836, I located a lot of land in the town of Farmington. To get on to this I had to go back half a mile without any road, cutting my way through bush. In the course of the season I erected a decent log cabin and moved to it in the fall, taking with one team, all our household furniture, and with another, lumber enough for part of a floor. With but part of a floor made of boards loosely thrown down, with blankets for doors and windows, we took possession.

Caleb's daughter Lydia Ann married Theodore P. Howard, who had come to Michigan in 1846 where he bought a farm on the shores of Orchard Lake. In order to supplement his farm earnings, Howard taught school in Farmington. It was here he met and was deeply moved by the Reverend Lamb:

> I also attended many excellent meetings here [in Farmington], one in particular, I shall remember long and well. It was on the evening of the 8th of March, when the good [Elder Lamb] preached a touching sermon, and poured out his whole soul for sinners. . . . I soon learned to pray, and took a stand among Christians, not afraid to show where I stood.

After marrying Lydia, the couple eventually sold their farm on Orchard Lake to purchase Caleb's farm where they settled on Twelve Mile and Halsted. Their life together was not an easy one. With nine children to raise and a farm to run, they worked hard to provide security for their family. The Howards raised sheep for their wool, and calves, which they sold in Detroit. They also grew apples and wheat. In addition to her mother's duties, Lydia Howard sold her own homemade butter and cider.

Howard traveled monthly to Detroit. Getting an early start, he would leave home at 4 a.m. with a large lantern fixed to the front of his wagon to light the way. Following the Plank Road, the 20-mile trip took about eight hours and cost about 83¢ in tolls. By noon, Howard would arrive at the market. Once his goods were sold, he would then shop for items and supplies he couldn't buy in Farmington before finally heading home.

Widely known as a devoted family man, Howard had some worldly advice for his sons:

> My dear boys—you are to promise before God—that you will put away all loud and angry talk to your parents and brothers and sisters—put

> away harsh words, and speak kindly to everybody and everything. Harsh words are like hailstones; destroy what they would nourish and sustain if they were melted into water. Agree not to quarrel let what will come, let each boy promise. I will give way if my brother won't—then keep your mouth shut and keep the hailstones in and there won't be much trouble.

He also left them with some practical instructions:

> For my boys—Always set posts top end in the ground. In laying over fence put a good stone or block under each corner, lay the best rails at the bottom. Keep all tools under shelter always. Every thing in its place then you will know where it is when you want it. Keep the stone walls all laid up even and the boards all nailed on. Do not carry in bags of meal on your best coat—nor do chores in your meeting pants—Lay stone walls north and south. Always have in view to work all loose stones into a wall sometime. Do not think about going away from home, home is the best place in the world.

Like their hardworking neighbors, the Howards knew their share of heartbreak. Late in 1859, they lost their 6-year-old twin boys Allen and Arthur, victims of "brain fever." Allen died first on December 15 and Arthur followed four days later. The boys are buried in the northwest part of West Farmington Cemetery under what was then a small oak tree, but has since grown to dominate the corner.

A grief-stricken father wrote to his family in New York:

> Our darling Allen has gone to rest, to sleep the sleep that knows no waking. . . . I saw his last expiring breath. I saw the fast flutter and sweet little Allen was all still, and now he is cold. Oh so cold. Oh it seems like a dream . . . God sustain us in this our affliction for our hearts are filled . . .
>
> Poor little Arthur; we have no trouble to keep his arms covered now. He died at 5:20. He never went to sleep easier apparently. Oh can it be. No it can't. He is now laid on the same board where his mate lay, and soon will lie by his side in the grave. . . . Oh how can we give him up . . . This is our first affliction, we have cried our eyes sore now and tomorrow we must see him put in the ground.

Edward Steele died in 1837. Shortly afterward, the Steele Sawmill burned. It went through a series of repairs until it finally fell into the hands of Mark Arnold and Warren Serviss, who ran the business for another ten years. The gristmill became not just the financial center of Sleepy Hollow, but the main gathering spot as well. Eventually, it fell under the ownership of John T. Little, who opened an adjacent store. A one-time sailor, Little renamed the mill "Pernambuco" after a port he had visited in Brazil. Pernambuco Flour was a local favorite and sold

The oak tree, a sapling when the Howard twins were laid to rest, now dominates the corner in West Farmington Cemetery. (Photo by Tim Ostrander.)

as far away as Detroit. The little town of Sleepy Hollow then became known as Pernambuco Hollow. A fire eventually put Little out of business and the Bank of Rochester foreclosed on his loan in 1851.

THE ENGLISH SETTLEMENT

Judah C. Marsch bought his property, located at the intersection of Thirteen Mile and Middlebelt Roads, directly from the government in 1824—the same year the Utleys arrived. Six years later, John T. Wilcox, known for enjoying a good drink, and his wife Mary, known to chase after him, purchased the land intending to farm. They also built the three-story John T. Wilcox Sawmill—a vital part of the English Settlement that stood until the 1980s when it was tore down due to neglect. A school was also built in the area and other businesses were established, among them a brick factory. Another community was taking root.

The brick factory and sawmill were owned and operated by Dorus Morton in 1833. Located at Inkster and Fourteen Mile Roads, the businesses were eventually

Handheld school bells, like the one pictured here from the 1800s, were used in the German and Nichols Schools. (Courtesy of the Farmington Community Library.)

bought by T.A. Bigelow. A man of Scottish descent, he came to Michigan after living in Canada. Renamed after its new owner, the Bigelow Sawmill burned down in 1873, but the Bigelow Brick Factory remained profitable. Bigelow Bricks were made from local clay deposits and can still be found in many of the older homes throughout Oakland County.

John and Grace German also settled in this area. They came here in 1830 from Beddelford, England, buying land that crossed Fourteen Mile in Farmington Township for $18 an acre. The Germans built a large Greek-Revival home made of Bigelow bricks. When their son George married Henrietta Pins in 1843, the newlyweds moved into the original house where they raised two sons and three daughters. The Germans donated part of their land along Middlebelt Road just south of Fourteen Mile for a school.

The German School was one of the best in the area, boasting several prominent instructors—among them Circuit Judge K.P. Rockwell, Attorney E.E. Humers, and Pontiac Postmaster Andrew Moore. Ten male teachers taught during the winter session, receiving $1,000 each, while one female instructor taught during the summer. She received a mere $400 for her services.

Another area within the English Settlement was known as Buckhorn Corners. Located at Twelve Mile and Inkster Roads, the unique name originated from a set of locked deer horns that hung on a post at the corner. Legend has it that the two bucks were fighting when Timothy Tolman and George Brownell, each carrying a shotgun, took aim and fired, simultaneously killing both deer. Finding it impossible to separate the intertwined antlers, the two men hung them up for all to see.

Tolman, a Scotsman, originally settled in the area in 1825. His cousin Nathaniel arrived in Farmington in 1826 where he married Mary Lewis. Their wedding, with Amos Mead officiating, was the first marriage celebrated in the township. The couple bought 80 acres of land from the government on what is now Eleven Mile and Middlebelt. Timothy Tolman, a carpenter by trade, built the first frame house in Farmington near Twelve Mile and Middlebelt in 1828.

George Brownell also came to Farmington in 1825, where he built a log cabin at Twelve Mile and Inkster. His brother John arrived the following year and settled nearby after marrying Esther Ingersoll. It was widely believed that the brothers owned land where a miraculous spring flowed, its water blessed with special healing powers.

Among the other newcomers to the English Settlement were George and Therina Tibbits, also native New Yorkers. Born in Wayne County, New York in 1802 and 1804, respectively, they were married in 1822. Two years later, they made their way to Michigan and settled on 160 acres of land in Farmington Township, for which they had papers signed by President James Monroe.

Like other pioneer couples, the Tibbits worked hard to clear their land and build a home, but unlike the others, they were college graduates who taught school back east. A firm believer in temperance, Tibbits raised the first frame barn in the township without benefit of whiskey—or so he thought. The other men had no qualms about sneaking alcohol to the site and, unbeknownst to George Tibbits, they enjoyed a few drinks while they worked. The barn was successfully raised without incident. Tibbits was so against drinking that he stubbornly refused to sell even one bushel of grain for the purpose of making whiskey or other such brew. Staunch Baptists and members of the Whig Party who later became Republicans, the couple had 11 children.

In 1828, the Tibbets built a sawmill in Buckhorn Corners alongside Lee's Creek. The Tibbits' Sawmill was not particularly successful and was eventually sold. George Tibbits died in 1856. His widow Therina then married the Reverend Nehemiah Lamb, founder of the First Baptist Church in Sleepy Hollow.

CLARENCEVILLE

In October 1830, Allen Weston bought 80 acres of land on the Grand River Trail in the extreme southeastern corner of the township near what is now Eight Mile Road. Weston himself lived in Howell and ran a tavern there. He sold the Farmington property to his brother Orrin, who built a house on the land in 1836. Two years later, and just one year after Michigan became a state, Allen Weston established a stagecoach line that ran from Howell to Detroit along the Grand

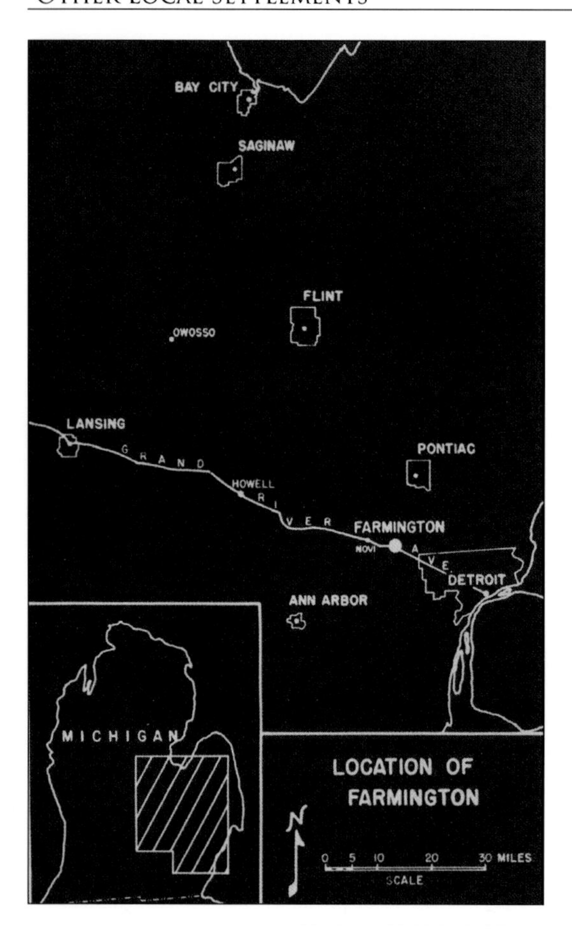

This map shows the location of Farmington between Detroit and Lansing. (Courtesy of the Farmington Community Library.)

River Trail. The new line brought more business to his brother's tavern, which happened to be located directly on the well-traveled route.

Three years later, the Weston brothers sold their property in both Howell and Farmington. Benjamin Spring bought the stage line as well as the tavern in Howell, while Stephen Jennings moved into the Farmington house on Grand River Trail. Jennings and his wife Polly ran the inn. They called it the Sixteen Mile House.

The *Oakland County History* of 1877 describes those early days:

> In the extreme southeastern corner of the township is a small cluster of buildings known as Clarenceville. It lies on the line of the Detroit and Howell plank-road, and it was to this thoroughfare, known in the early days as the Grand River Military Road, that the hamlet owes its existence. Its commencement was the building of a tavern at that point by Stephen Jennings, in the year 1836, for the accommodation of the travel over the road. He also opened a store there soon after. During all the days of staging over this road Jennings' tavern was a regular and favorite stopping-place, the sixteen-mile station out from Detroit.

In 1847, another fortuitous event affected the township—Lansing replaced Detroit as Michigan's state capitol. Now it was imperative that an even better road be built leading from Detroit to Lansing. The original military road was unkempt and muddy, filled with ruts. With approximately 124 wagons a day traveling to and from Detroit, the road was much too hazardous and narrow to handle the increase in traffic. Therefore, in 1848, the state legislature passed the General Plank Road Law. This act provided for the construction of plank toll roads between Detroit and Lansing, as well as Detroit and Pontiac. Once again, Farmington was in the right place at the right time and so was the Sixteen Mile House, now owned and operated by John Claugherty.

The original Grand River Military Road traveled from Detroit to Redford before passing through Farmington and on to Howell. The new road followed the same route as today's Grand River Avenue. The original military road was abandoned except for a small stretch of Nine Mile. The new plank road was 16 feet wide with a shoulder running along each side. Money to upkeep the road was obtained through tolls. A tollgate was established every 5 miles and the charge was 1¢ per mile for a sled, sleigh, or rider, while a wagon pulled by two or more horses paid 2¢. Anyone refusing to pay the toll was fined $25.

The Sixteen Mile House was strategically located at the Fourth Toll Gate. With Claugherty in charge, a small town known as Clarenceville prospered around it.

This tollhouse is believed to have been located on Grand River Plank Road at Inkster. (Courtesy of the Farmington Community Library.)

Dedicated to servicing travelers who came by horseback and stagecoach along the new plank road, the settlement thrived.

The Grand River Plank Road was a vast improvement over its predecessor. Comprised of oak planks measuring 3 inches thick and 12 feet long, it passed 800 feet south of Farmington. Completed in 1851, it wasn't long before the new plank road became one of Michigan's main thoroughfares. With only a single lane, all Detroit-bound traffic had the right of way. Anyone driving in the opposite direction had to move over—even if it meant getting stuck in the mud.

Claugherty owned the Sixteen Mile House for 15 years, after which a succession of new proprietors tried running it without much luck. It took Milton Botsford, an experienced innkeeper and businessman, to see that the inn reached its full potential. Botsford was the oldest son of Farmington's Lemuel and Lucy Botsford. Originally from Connecticut, they were drawn to the small community in Michigan founded by fellow Quakers.

In 1836, the Botsfords bought land in Section 22 of Farmington Township on what came to be known as Botsford Hill. A small house and barn were already built upon the site, but Lemuel erected a much larger house near today's Ten Mile and Farmington Roads. The oversized white house still serves as a private residence. The Botsfords' eldest son Milton, who married Lovinia Phelps from Pennsylvania, ran the Coach House directly across the street from his parents'

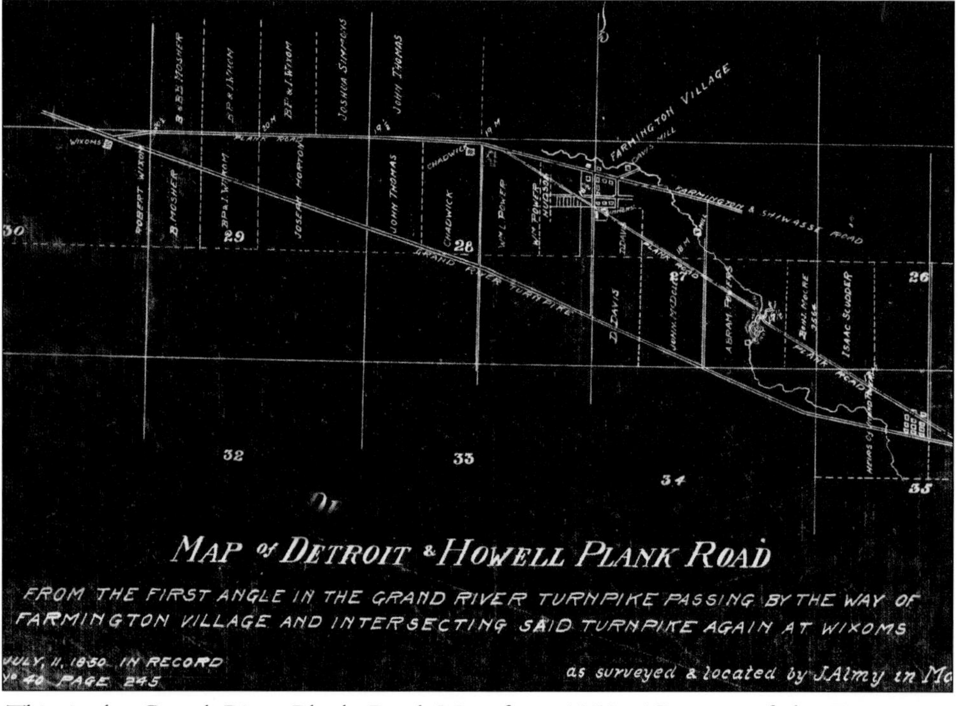

This is the Grand River Plank Road Map from 1850. (Courtesy of the Farmington Community Library.)

The Botsford House on Botsford Hill is at Ten Mile and Farmington Roads. (Courtesy of the Farmington Community Library.)

home. The Coach House served travelers heading to Pontiac along the Orchard Lake Trail. A Jacksonian Democrat, Lemuel served as commissioner of highways in addition to raising ten children, including Milton, who purchased the Sixteen Mile House just prior to the Civil War.

Renamed the Botsford Inn, it became known as one of the territory's finest establishments. Besides having a large second-floor ballroom, the inn boasted an elegant parlor, as well as a formal dining room for highbrow ladies and gentlemen as they were passing through. In contrast, there was also a common taproom with its own entrance. Here the drovers, considered riff-raff, came with their herds as they traveled to market. Corrals where hundreds of sheep and cattle could spend the night were located out back. Since it took two or three days to drive a flock into Detroit, Friday nights always seemed to be the busiest. The drovers would stop for the night, buy cheap drinks, and sleep on the floor.

The more refined clientele got fancy food and expensive liquor in the dining room. The stagecoach, normally filled with passengers, made a daily stop at the Botsford Inn for lunch. Dances were held in the ballroom beginning at 3 p.m. Various bands played music until five the next morning for the guests' enjoyment. Floor managers patrolled the area making sure the drovers stayed out. For the upper echelon, carriage houses were located behind the inn and stalls reserved for their horses.

In addition to the inn, a general store was also opened in Clarenceville, along with a wagon shop, two blacksmiths, and a post office. Local businesses thrived as the number of travelers coming and going to the new state capitol increased.

NORTH FARMINGTON

Another major settlement, known as North Farmington, was located at Farmington Road between Thirteen and Fourteen Mile. It was the place where Chauncey Wolcott first chose to settle when he came to Farmington in 1827. Wolcott ran a store at Thirteen Mile and Farmington Roads. His father John soon followed, but died in 1830 and was buried behind the Wolcott house. Wolcott, John Button, and Orange Culver officially organized the small village of North Farmington in 1837—the same year Michigan became a state. They established the Wolcott Cemetery and the body of John Wolcott was moved there.

Known today as North Farmington Cemetery, a veteran from every American war is buried there. One such man, Levi Green, enlisted to serve his fledgling country on July 1, 1776. He fought valiantly at the Battle of Bunker Hill during the Revolutionary War. He collected an annual pension of $23.32 from the War Department for being a Revolutionary soldier. The Green family, also early Farmington settlers, owned a powder horn that Levi carried with him in battle. It was inscribed as follows:

> Levi Green, His Horn, Who Enlisted in the Continental Service to Range in the County of Albany in the Year 1776 under Leftenant Jackson During the Congress

The Button family, originally from Connecticut, also took up residence in North Farmington. After a move to Pennsylvania, John and Cynthia Button decided to head further west, so they purchased the northeast corner of Section 4 in May 1828. John's cousin, 19-year-old Charles Bissel Button, came to Farmington in 1829, settling in the southwest quarter of Section 9 where he purchased land from George C. Taylor for $121. Eleven years later, John Button was a representative in the state legislature along with Milton Botsford.

From 1825 to 1826, Orange Culver and his brother George bought land in Section 10 where they built a log cabin. By 1835, Orange Culver had sold his portion of the land and purchased another 80 acres from the Oakland County Treasurer for $192. This parcel of land was located on Fourteen Mile and Farmington Roads. Here, Orange Culver built a four-room house with two floors, part of which still stands today.

Although North Farmington didn't grow quite as large as the other local settlements, the small town prospered. It served as a transportation center for those traveling north into Pontiac, as well as those traveling south where they picked up the old plank road on their way to either Lansing or Detroit. By 1847, a post office was established at Wolcott Corners with Chauncey Wolcott appointed first postmaster. With grocery stores and blacksmith shops, Wolcott Corners was most famous for the large elm tree that grew right in the middle of the road. The tree itself, a local landmark, withstood storms, ice, winds, and automobiles, but finally succumbed to Dutch Elm Disease in the early 1960s. Almost 90 inches in diameter, it was estimated to be about 300 years old.

As the Upper Rouge River wound its way through Farmington Township and became a vital part of the various settlements, it supported the many sawmills and gristmills that sprung up in the area. Businesses grew around these mills. Churches, cemeteries, and schools were also established as people came together out of a basic need to form communities, thereby improving their lifestyles and ensuring their future.

With Quakertown as the main district, the small towns joined together to face the future as the climate of the country changed with talk of a Civil War. The citizens of Farmington united and once again rose to the challenge. Disregarding their own fears, they chose to make a difference by righting a terrible wrong. They took risks for a national cause they believed in and dug in their heels when faced with a catastrophe that struck them personally. The people of Farmington were a hardy lot who knew what had to be done and simply did it.

The grave of Revolutionary War soldier Levi Green is in North Farmington Cemetery. (Photo by Tim Ostrander.)

4. The Railroad, the War, and the Fire

The anti-slavery movement was born back east where many of Michigan's settlers originated. Religious people like the Quakers deplored the living and working conditions forced upon the slaves. They passionately campaigned for the abolishment of such treatment. Therefore, it was no surprise to find their Farmington counterparts taking a stand as well. In 1836, the Michigan State Anti-Slavery Society was formed. Farmington's own Nathan Power was one of the 11 vice presidents, as well as president of the Oakland County Anti-Slavery Society. Power mentions attending several anti-slavery meetings in his diary. No less inspiring was the infamous slave Sojourner Truth, who spoke several times right here in Farmington on behalf of her people.

After a while, casting votes and giving speeches weren't enough. Escaped slaves needed tangible help in order to remain free. Many of them fled to Michigan and were eventually taken to Canada where their freedom wasn't challenged. As angry slave owners chased down their runaway slaves, violence often erupted. Something had to be done and so, in 1850, the Fugitive Slave Law was passed, making it illegal for anyone to help escaping slaves.

According to the law, slaves were no more than property; therefore, anyone assisting a slave would be found guilty of stealing. If caught, these unlucky heroes risked not only a $1,000 fine, but prison time as well. There were those daring individuals, however, who simply could not turn their backs on such desperate people. As a result, a finely-tuned system known as the Underground Railroad evolved, covertly carrying slaves to safety. Although there are no written records concerning Farmington's involvement with fugitive slaves, local legend has it that the people of Farmington took part the in clandestine affair. It was something they just didn't talk about.

The leg of the "railroad" that stopped in Farmington began down south, traveling northward through Ohio to Michigan and then on to Canada. Travel began around 1836 and continued throughout the Civil War years. Thousands of slaves followed the route seeking freedom. "Conductors" escorted them hidden in wagons beneath hay or produce. Often they stopped at various "stations"

The Philbrick Tavern, owned by Nathan Philbrick, was one of the finest hostels in Oakland County. Located at Eleven Mile and Power Roads, the tavern served as a meeting place for the early township government, possibly a station along the Underground Railroad, and is now a private residence. (Courtesy of the Farmington Community Library.)

along the way until it was safe for them to travel on. These stations were about 15 miles apart.

Michigan's main route passed south of Farmington, but when travel on this path was jeopardized, an alternative northern route was taken. This included stops in Farmington, where it is believed that Nathan Power himself was a conductor and that his home, the former Quaker meetinghouse, was a station. Of course, he didn't act alone. There were many others in Farmington who also took part—among them, Nathan's brothers Ira and Abram, as well as Chauncy Green and John Thayer. In addition to Power's home, the Philbrick Tavern and the First Baptist Church were also rumored to be just some of the stations along the route of the Underground Railroad as it passed through Farmington.

It was risky, but a hardworking farmer—especially a religious one—taking his goods to Detroit roused little suspicion. Who would have thought that his wagon full of wares secretly carried a runaway slave or two? Once in the big city, there were two main stations in the downtown area: the Second Baptist Church of Detroit at Monroe and Beaubien (now part of today's Greektown) and the Finney House Barn, a hotel at the corner of State and Griswold. It wasn't uncommon for conductors such as Nathan Power to stop at the Finney and inconspicuously unload their cargo.

Abram Power's son John was just a child during those difficult years, but he described what he remembered in an article written for the *Detroit News* in 1909:

> We children had never heard of the "underground railway" and did not know for a long time what was going on, but we felt that a mystery had suddenly been laid over the place. Occasionally, early in the morning, and at different times of the day, we would see mother coming from the barn with an empty dish or plate. We would be cautioned to stay away from the barn for a few days, and then things would be all right again. Childlike, we would want to know the reason for it all, but would only receive some evasive answer to each of our questions.
>
> However, when we grew older, we learned that on those occasions, there was a Negro slave being concealed in the barn until such a time that it was deemed safe to send him over the border into Canada, where he would be free. When a safe time would arrive, my father would hitch up to a load of hay or grain, conceal the slave somewhere in the load and drive down to the docks at Detroit, and when all was ready, the Negro would slip off the load, get into a boat, and be quickly ferried across to Windsor, where no master's hands could be laid on him.

Aaron and Ellen Wilson were two such slaves running for their lives. It was their second attempt at gaining freedom. The first time, they were captured and returned to their owner in Freemont, Virginia. They vowed that the next time would be different. That's when the couple, along with three other slaves, stole their mistress's horse and traveled to Michigan. Their owners caught up with them, but this time the runaways fought back and escaped for good. Passing through Farmington on their way to Windsor, the Wilsons liked what they saw. After living for a time in Canada, the couple returned to Farmington. They settled on 5 acres at what is now Eleven Mile and Orchard Lake Roads, becoming Farmington's only African-Canadian-American family. Aaron died in 1908. When Ellen died tragically five years later, her demise made front-page news in *The Farmington Enterprise*:

> Mrs. Wilson, who slept near the stove, got up Tuesday morning and started a fire in the stove and went back to bed. In a short time, the fire burned too briskly and the old lady attempted to turn the damper in the pipe, when her clothes caught fire. She shouted "fire," and the daughter rushed to her assistance with a pail of water, which she threw over her mother, and prevented her burning to death.
>
> A physician was called and her burns were dressed and she was made as comfortable as possible, but the shock and her extreme age, which is said to be over 100 years, caused her death Thursday morning.

The Wilsons' daughter Emma married Darius Hullm and moved to Detroit. The Hullms had a son, Wellington, who temporarily came to live with Emma's sister Mary in Farmington. He ended up staying for good. To help her nephew fit in with the locals, Mary promptly changed his first name to Pete. Pete attended the local public schools and graduated from Farmington High in 1928. He found work repairing radios and eventually took on televisions. After serving in World War II, Hullm returned to his home in Farmington where he married his wife Helen and raised three children, Tracey, Adrianne, and Dwight.

While the men and women of Farmington helped the runaway slaves, the climate of the country was changing. Talk of a Civil War began to infiltrate everyday life. Even incoming Michigan governor Austin Blair spoke of it during his inaugural address in 1861: "Secession is revolution and revolution in the overt act is treason and must be treated as such."

Pete Hullm's grandmother Ellen Wilson was a former slave. (Courtesy of the Farmington Community Library.)

Wellington (Pete) Hullm is shown here as a boy, c. 1915. (Courtesy of the Farmington Community Library.)

Based on Blair's recommendations, the state legislature passed a resolution that pledged Michigan's military power and resources to the United States government. Therefore it was no surprise when, after the attack on Fort Sumter off the South Carolina coast, Blair received a telegram from President Abraham Lincoln requesting assistance from Michigan. The very first man to enlist was Farmington's own A.J. Crosby Jr.

Born in New York in 1840, Crosby came to Michigan with his parents, A.J. Sr. and Lurania, along with two brothers, when he was only four. The Crosbys farmed in Livonia for the next 11 years, before buying an improved farm in Farmington Township. Crosby attended Farmington schools before going on to Detroit's Bryant and Stratton's Business College, where he became an assistant teacher after completing his education. Heeding the president's call, 20-year-old Crosby rushed to the Detroit Light Guard, signed up for a three-month stay, and became the first soldier in Michigan to enlist for Civil War duty.

Along with 797 other soldiers assigned to the first company of the first regiment from Michigan, Crosby left for Washington, D.C. on May 16, 1861. Wearing navy blue and gray uniforms, the men carried Model 1855 Springfield muskets. The people of Washington, afraid of an imminent Confederate attack, were relieved to see them. President Lincoln himself was quoted as saying, "Thank God for Michigan." The troops immediately went to work in Virginia taking back Alexandria. Right after that, Crosby grew ill with dysentery and pleurisy. Before the month was over, he was hospitalized.

By the time his three-month stint was up, Crosby was too ill to re-enlist. Instead of staying with his battalion, he returned to his parents' farm in Farmington. The following year, he married Mary B. Smith of Novi and eventually moved to St. Johns, Michigan where he resumed his teaching career. The Crosbys had three children, a son and two daughters. Although he no longer lived in the township, Crosby became a member of the Masonic Fraternity and belonged to Farmington's Lodge No. 151. On November 9, 1909, as he was standing on a corner in downtown Farmington conversing with Governor Fred Warner, Crosby lit a cigar and collapsed. He was dead at the age of 69, still proud of his unique status as Michigan's first Civil War soldier.

Edwin Parker was another local Civil War veteran. Married to Arthur Power's daughter Esther, Parker belonged to Michigan's Fourth Cavalry, reputedly a tough battalion. So tough, in fact, that once the war was over, they were sent to capture Confederate president Jefferson Davis, now on the run. In hot pursuit, Michigan's Fourth, along with Wisconsin's First Cavalry, gave chase. The troops finally caught up with Davis near Irwinville, Georgia. Edwin Parker was among the four men assigned as Davis's prison-escort. During their journey, the two adversaries became friends. In appreciation of Parker's kindness, Davis gave him a set of his spurs, along with a pair of his gloves.

Also in Michigan's Fourth Cavalry was another Farmington son, Caleb W. Horton. Enlisting in August 1862, Horton found himself part of the Army of the Cumberland. He was taken prisoner at the Battle of Mission Ridge in 1863 and ultimately ended up at Andersonville, where he spent the better part of 1864. Eventually, he was released as part of a prisoner exchange program. Honorably discharged and paid off by the government, he returned to Farmington where he began a career in the mercantile business.

But there were more. Based on Lincoln's request, one regiment was to be formed from each of Michigan's six congressional districts. Although additional companies followed, these original regiments were identified as the 18th through 23rd Michigan Infantries. The 22nd Infantry was assigned to Michigan's Fifth Congressional District, which included Oakland, Livingston, Macomb, St. Clair, Lapeer, and Sanilac Counties. As many as 997 men gathered for service at Pontiac on August 29, 1862—among them young men from Farmington. Five days later, under the command of former governor Moses Wisner, the 22nd left for Kentucky after a colorful send-off from the ladies of Pontiac.

William H. Wiend, a volunteer from Farmington, recalled that day in an article he wrote for the local *Enterprise* newspaper in 1930:

> Sixty-four years ago, September 4th, the 22nd Michigan Infantry, commanded by Governor Moses Wisner, left Pontiac for the front, Captain E.C. Hatton commanded Company A, the first of ten companies

> to report at camp with full quota of 100 men, or rather boys, as over one half were under nineteen years of age.
>
> In that company were about fifteen Farmington boys . . . Daniel Snyder, 42; Franklin Knowlton, 38; and Joseph Lamb, about 25; 1st Sergeant George Button, 22. The others were, if memory serves me right, all under twenty: William Smith, Hudson Wilcox, Henry Knapp, Jesse Sage, Charles Wiend, William Seaton, Lyman Heath, and William Wiend, who later proved to be the youngest of the regiment, just seventeen, until little Johnny Clem, now Major-General John L. Clem, U.S.A., enlisting in February, at the age of eleven years and six months, deprived me of that distinction.
>
> Almost seventy years have rolled away since we marched down Saginaw Street to the old Detroit and Milwaukee depot, where the long train was waiting to bear us away to the Southland. The street and sidewalks were crowded with fathers, mothers, sisters and brothers and friends, watching to catch the last glimpse of their son or brother. And today I am the last one of that Farmington squad, left waiting the last great roll call, eight of whom were schoolmates of mine in the little Red School house at West Farmington.
>
> How well I remember those boy schoolmates and later comrades, not one of whom was twenty years old. They did not volunteer because drums were beating, flags flying and crowds cheering. It was the darkest year of the War for the Union. President Lincoln had just issued the call . . . to save the Union, and the young boys of the country answered, most of them boys from the farms still in their teens.
>
> No bounties offered and pay $13 a month, but they did not hesitate though they well knew only hard marching, long weary nights on the dangerous picket, fast and hard fighting waited them at the front. I sometimes wonder if the boys of today ever stop to think what it cost to save the Union from 1861 to 1865.

Filled with enthusiasm and anxious to defend the Union, Farmington's soldiers, like most others, left their homes in anticipation of what they viewed as their "great adventure." Reality soon shifted their mode of thinking as they spent day after day in never-ending drills and monotonous marching. They endured bad weather, gnawing hunger, and extreme sickness. Moses Wisner himself died in Lexington, Kentucky on January 4, 1863, a victim of typhoid fever.

Later that year, the 22nd found themselves 12 miles south of Chattanooga in the midst of the Battle at Chickamauga (Georgia) where they suffered the heaviest losses of any Union battalion. It was here that their drummer, "Little Johnny Clem," distinguished himself. An orphan originally from Ohio, Clem was a small boy who stood under 4 feet tall and weighed less than 70 pounds.

On the morning of September 20, 1863, the 22nd started out 584 men strong. Clem, in a specially made uniform to fit his pint-sized stature, was given the

This memorial was erected in 1923 behind the town hall. Farmington Civil War veterans are listed above the Spanish-American War veterans. (Photo by Tom Ostrander.)

job of marking formation lines. During the course of the day, the youngster abandoned his assignment, choosing to pick up a musket and fight alongside his company. By nightfall, the 197 men that remained found themselves surrounded by Confederates, who ordered them to surrender. Not one to give up, Clem took aim and shot a Confederate colonel right out of his saddle. More shots were exchanged and three bullets pierced Clem's hat, narrowly missing his head.

While many were taken prisoner that night, including their commander, Colonel Heber Le Favour, Clem lay quietly on the battlefield where he was left for dead. Under the cover of darkness, he slipped through enemy lines and found his way back to what was left of his regiment. For his heroics, he was appointed sergeant. After the war, he returned to civilian life where he completed his high school education before enrolling at West Point. Clem was appointed cadet-at-large in 1871 by President Ulysses S. Grant and commissioned as a second lieutenant. By the time he retired from military life in 1916, he reached the rank of major general and was a source of pride to the men of Michigan's 22nd Infantry, whom he so gallantly fought beside.

In the end, the 22nd mustered out of Nashville, but not before they marched into Atlanta under the leadership of General Sherman. Those whose enlistments were not over were transferred to the 29th Michigan Infantry, while the rest were paid off and sent back to Detroit. The troop lost a total of 399 men—89 were killed or mortally wounded in battle, while 310 died of disease.

Despite their missing menfolk, life back in Michigan remained much the same. The older men, women, and children who were left behind maintained the farms. New-fangled machines such as threshers and reapers became the norm. The ladies formed "Aid Societies," gathering together to prepare bandages and clothes for their men at the front while raising money for the soldiers' relief fund. Business boomed as prices steadily rose. Wages, however, stayed at a minimum.

Gardurous Webster, a Farmington resident whose grandfather fought in the Revolutionary War under General Lafayette, owned a harness shop on Grand River and Liberty Street. Established in 1844, his was just one of the many businesses that profited from the war years. A staunch Methodist known for his excellent work, he contracted with the War Department to provide the cavalry with harnesses. This lucrative deal allowed him to employ several local men who needed work.

The following article appeared in the *Detroit Free Press* on March 5, 1864:

> Three years ago a man could support his family well on $600 a year. An article of dress or furniture costs at least twice what it did then. Flour

Grand Army of the Republic (GAR) Veterans of the Civil War and their spouses posed for this group shot, c. 1899, in front of the town hall. (Courtesy of the Farmington Community Library.)

and meat from 25 to 35 percent more. Wood then $3 per cord, now costs $6 or $7. Coffee then 20 cents per pound and now 45 cents. Sugar at 8 to 12 cents now 17 to 20. Butter 10 to 12 cents now is thirty. Potatoes could be had for 5 cents per bushel, they now cost that per peck. Onions which sold at 40 cents per bushel are now $2.50. Eggs once sold for 10 cents per dozen, now 20 is the lowest figure. Groceries of all kinds have advanced at least 5 percent and some as much as 100 percent.

Time was when respectable board could be had for $3 per week. Now attics will stand empty before they will be rented for less than $4 or $5 and from this prices range upward to $30, $40, $50 per month.

The carefully kept farm records of Theodore P. Howard give us a glimpse of economic life in Farmington in 1864:

December 31—Year end total:

Wheat raised	17 bu	
Oats	165 bu	
Potatoes	80 bu	
Corn	400 bu	
Sold in 1864:	Produce	$316.90
	Stock/produce	$549.50
		$866.40
	For goods and groceries	$128.72
	Leaving a year's profit at:	$737.68

Too old to enlist himself, Howard, like many other locals, was still personally affected by the nation's call to arms. His younger brother Lewis joined the 51st New York Volunteers. Louis died from disease on August 30, 1863 in Covington, Kentucky. An undated letter written by Theodore to his brother describes the sentiment of many northerners during these turbulent times:

I am glad our father's family can furnish at least one Soldier to fight for our country. If ever there was a time when men should show their true colors it is now. Now, when our loved country is besieged by a horde of slave holding out-laws ready to trample in the dust and destroy forever the flag that has been honored and respected, ever since our nation had its birth. It is not enough to make one's blood curdle in his veins to thinking "Lexington" where our loved flag was trailed and trampled in the dust by the rebels.

Howard also had a younger sister, Elizabeth, who had been a missionary in Haiti. Now a member of the Virginia Freedman's Relief Association, she taught ex-slaves in Lynchburg. After the war, she wrote a letter to her brother in Farmington dated October 28, 1866:

> I came here from Washington the 10th [of October] to teach Men's schools. We found schools in the town already organized and under the care of detailed soldiers and two young men who commenced teaching while soldiers were adopted by our Society after they were mustered out of military service. We board with two ladies who although southern, are very strong Union antislavery women. . . . Our school is in the lower part of an old Tobacco Factory now used by the colored people for church. It is very cold and open and damp. . . . Lynchburg is a famous old Secesh town and the Rebels succeeded in holding the place during the war. After Lee's surrender the soldiers came here and some of them were butchered in cold blood. Two thousand of our men were kept here as prisoners of war and were guarded by pickets placed on the hills around the mud hole where our boys were kept.

Young John Power was another local man looking for adventure. In July 1863, he left Farmington for New York City where he saw violence unlike anything he'd ever witnessed back home. While there, he watched as the "Plug Uglies," a New York gang, erupted into violence and saw firsthand the burning of a "Negro orphanage." It prompted him to join the Navy. Power was assigned to the U.S.S. *North Carolina*, but three weeks later transferred to the U.S.S. *Pensacola*. While on board, he came down with yellow fever and was sent to a marine hospital. Once recovered, he was given the job of hospital steward and cared for other soldiers stricken with the same disease. Eventually, he returned to the *Pensacola* before being sent to the *Monongahela* under the command of "Old Iron Admiral Farragut." This time, Power was appointed paymaster's steward—a position he held until the *Monongahela* went out of commission after the war.

Power also saw his share of action. He fought in tempestuous battles, including that of Mobile Bay. He witnessed the surrender of Fort Gains, Fort Powell, and Fort Morgan. Upon his discharge, Power returned to Michigan via the Grand Trunk Railroad in the midst of the country's celebration of the Union's victory and the end of civil strife.

Newspaper headlines carried the news of General Lee's surrender. Businesses were closed as the euphoric mood spread from city to city. Thousands gathered together, enthusiastically rejoicing the war's end. They played music, lit bonfires, and decorated their homes and businesses with a patriotic flair. Their joyous mood, however, was soon transformed into somber shock as news of Lincoln's assassination hit home less than one week later.

Nathan Power made the trip to Washington to attend the slain president's funeral. He described the pulse of the nation that day:

> I attended . . . the funeral of Abraham Lincoln who was assassinated on the evening of 14th of 4th month by a pistol shot by some ruffian. This was the most melancholy event ever happening in our country. The wail of feeling and sorrow was deep throughout all the land. . . . The whole was a solemn scene of deep interest to us all.

Our soldiers came home, forever changed physically and emotionally: some minus an arm or a leg or both, some still recovering from bullet wounds and sickness, and others bore scars that couldn't be seen. Their great adventure now over, new challenges faced them as they tried to pick up the lives they left behind. On August 2, 1865, Power wrote of their bittersweet homecoming:

> Was a day set apart by this and adjoining towns to Welcome the Soldiers home from the terrible four years War. They met in the Stephen Lapham Maple Grove. Three thousand people were supposed to be present. . . . So ends our terrible war in April 1865 which has abolished slavery in our entire country. It was done in a way the South chose and willed to have it in an attempt to strengthen it. We feel that more has passed during the four years gone by than usually transpires in 200 years. . . . The ball is in motion to restore to man his Inalienable rights everywhere. Twenty-three young men have been lost in this war from our town.

John Power (1844–1924) fought in the Battle of Mobile Bay before joining a traveling theater group. (Courtesy of the Farmington Community Library.)

P. Dean Warner, who served as a Michigan senator and did much to shape Farmington, was elected first president when Farmington became a village in 1867. (Courtesy of the Farmington Community Library.)

Overall, Michigan paid a heavy toll—of the 90,000 men sent to battle, 14,000 died—mostly from disease.

In the years following the war, the country experienced a "boom" both economically and developmentally. Michigan and Farmington were no exception. Here, most local farms made their livelihood by growing grain for market, as well as domestic use. As a result of this unprecedented period of growth, the township was incorporated and, in 1867, officially became the Village of Farmington. "Quakertown" was a thing of the past. The new village encompassed 1 square mile of Farmington centered around Grand River and Farmington Roads. Elected to office on May 6, 1867 were trustees Justus B. Webster, Anson J. Cloyse, and George Matthews. P. Dean Warner, formerly known as Pascal D'Angelis, was voted president.

The first ordinance passed by the village council established a pound where stray animals were kept until claimed by their owners. The pound master was often the target of angry citizens, but the council always defended him no matter how many hogs, geese, ducks, sheep, and goats were rounded up from the city streets. Exempt from the new rules were cows giving milk. They were allowed to roam freely from six in the morning until seven in the evening, but only during the months of May through November.

As council president, P. Dean Warner was one of Farmington's most influential citizens. He wore many hats as a local businessman and politician. In addition to being a private banker, he partnered up with his wife's brother Myron Botsford (now married to Arthur Power's youngest daughter Duana). The two men opened a general store in the business district. In addition to his private duties, Warner, a Democrat, was elected to the Michigan State Senate in 1850 where he served as speaker of the House.

Warner introduced a resolution that would give African-American residents of the state the right to vote. The resolution was resoundingly voted down 32,026 to 12,840. Completely against the issue of slavery and a staunch supporter of equality, Warner left the Democratic Party prior to the Civil War to become a Republican and campaign for Abraham Lincoln. Elected to the Michigan House of Representatives in 1864, he served on various committees for Ways and Means and Internal Improvements. Reelected in 1866, he represented several townships, including Bloomfield, West Bloomfield, Royal Oak, Southfield, and his hometown, Farmington.

Married to Rhoda Botsford on November 8, 1845, the childless couple eventually adopted a daughter, Mary Elizabeth Jones, in 1859, and a son, Frederick Maltby, in 1865, who was only three months old. The boy, born in England, lost

The large house built by P. Dean Warner on Grand River is now home to the Farmington Historical Museum. (Photo by Tim Ostrander.)

his mother just as the Maltbys arrived in Livonia. Warner took him in and saw to it that Fred received a good education. Once Fred completed the eighth grade in Farmington, he briefly attended the Michigan Agricultural College (now Michigan State University). After that, his father personally trained him in the mercantile business. When Fred turned 21, P. Dean literally handed over the store, which allowed him to pursue his own interest in banking. Three years later, Fred expanded the family business to include a hardware store next door.

In between his business enterprises, his public service, and raising his children, P. Dean Warner built a large white Victorian mansion that stood guard over 7 acres of land just west of the village. Construction of the five-bedroom home began in 1867 and was completed two years later. Featuring a water tank on top and two and a half baths inside, it was the first home in Farmington to boast indoor plumbing. The Warner House is still located on the south side of Grand River and is currently home to the Farmington Historical Museum.

Farmington also had its very own connection to the Wild West. Olive Oatman was literally one of Farmington's more colorful characters. In 1851, her family headed west to California on the Santa Fe Trail. As they neared New Mexico's Fort Yuma on the banks of the Gila River, Apache Indians attacked them. They murdered Oatman's parents and kidnapped her and her sister. After several years of living among the Native Americans, local resident Henry Grinell orchestrated her rescue, but not before the Apache tattooed her chin with parallel blue lines.

This barn-turned-garage is next to the Warner Mansion. Note the plaque that bears the name "P. Dean Warner" and the year 1867. (Photo by Tim Ostrander.)

This gazebo, on the grounds of the Warner Mansion, has become a customary location to take prom and wedding pictures. (Photo by Tim Ostrander.)

Settling in Farmington, Oatman often visited the schoolchildren to relate her exciting story.

As a new decade approached, the Village of Farmington flourished. According to the census of 1870, 400 people lived in the village itself with 2,170 living throughout the township. There was a total of 16,514 acres of farmland worth over $1 million. Livestock was valued at just under $200,000, including 642 horses, 1,117 cows, 22 oxen, 5,378 sheep, and 1,060 pigs. A total of 43,643 bushels of spring and winter wheat were harvested, along with 38,175 bushels of Indian corn, 39,127 bushels of oats, and 36,780 bushels of potatoes. Average workers were paid approximately $1 for a 12- to 15-hour day, while skilled tradesmen such as carpenters earned 15¢ an hour and brick masons, 20¢.

During the 1870s, the Detroit, Lansing, and Lake Michigan Railroad ran from Detroit just south of Farmington through Livonia and Plymouth on its way to Lansing. As railroad travel replaced stagecoach travel, the Grand River Plank Road saw less and less traffic. Even though tolls were still being charged, the road was not maintained. Left in disrepair, the oak planks shifted and bellowed, making the now muddy road bumpy and hard to maneuver. Due to the inconvenience and lengthy travel time, most travelers chose to ride the railroad. This meant a decrease in business for the local taverns and stores established on Grand River, but not before disaster of another kind struck.

With the summer of 1872 being one of excessive drought, the constant threat of fire hung in the parched air. By fall, the dry earth grew even dryer. At 2 a.m. on October 9, 1872, the unthinkable happened—a fire broke out in O.B. Smith Drygoods Store on the north side of Grand River just east of Farmington Road. As the fire rapidly spread, raging from one building to the next, the townspeople rallied together. With no established fire department and only two wells to draw from, the volunteer bucket brigade soon ran out of water. The fire rapidly raced down the main road, taking several businesses and homes with it.

It was Chauncey Green who came to the rescue, riding on horseback from his farm on Nine Mile Road. From atop his horse, he instructed the frenzied firefighters to tear down a house directly in the fire's path. Ropes were attached to the timbers while men and women alike pulled with all their might. The house came tumbling down and the debris was hauled away as quickly as possible, leaving a gaping space that the fire couldn't jump. Green's quick thinking and clever idea saved the day as the fire, with nowhere to go, finally burned itself out. Ten buildings were lost, including the drygoods store where the Masonic and Township meetings were regularly held on the second floor. Township records were destroyed, along with a shoe shop, a millinery shop, a drugstore, a jewelry store, and a blacksmith shop.

As the village swept up the ashes and removed the charred debris, Nathan Power mourned. That summer, 76-year-old Patience fell in the parlor, breaking her hip. After suffering for over 40 days, she died in September 1872, just weeks before the great fire devastated Grand River. No stranger to hard times, Power wrote of her passing:

> She was buried on the third day after her death. . . . Funeral was held at our dwelling at 11 o'clock. Was sung at the open grave, *Shall We Gather at the River*. We had been married 38 years, 6 months and 12 days. She made a peaceful and Christian close of life. . . . It was now on my getting home that I felt exceeding lonesome. Patience place was vacant, the house was void of her company. . . . So we are passing away. I endeavor to stay my mind on him who spake and it steadfast who is strength in weakness and a present help in the time of need.

Power survived her for almost a year and a half. His death on January 20, 1874 marked the end of an era in Farmington's history, but the village his father founded 50 years before was remarkably resilient. Despite the devastating blow to businessmen like P. Dean Warner, the Village of Farmington rallied to rebuild its community. Digging in their heels, the residents started over. They hadn't come this far to give up now.

5. REBUILDING

It was a time of dirt roads, wooden outhouses, and kerosene lamps. Electricity, telephones, and central heat were practically unheard of. When they weren't walking, Farmington residents rode horses or pedaled bicycles. Clothes were washed on a scrub board and meals were cooked on oil, wood, or coal stoves. Carpets were swept with a broom when they weren't hung outside and whipped into shape with a rug beater. One-room schools throughout the township numbered ten. Travelers boarded at either the Botsford Inn or the Owen House where $1 rented them a room for the night.

The Owen House, formerly the Swan Hotel, was a popular stopping place on the southeast corner of Grand River and Farmington Road. A first-class hotel in its day, the owner and permanent tenant, Lewis "Daff" Owen, was known for miles as an exceptional host who spared no expense when it came to his guests. Originally born in Romeo, Michigan in 1841, Owen came to Farmington in 1870 after serving in the Fifth Michigan Infantry during the Civil War. According to the *Oakland County Portrait and Biographical Album*, Owen was a genuine war hero. During his three-year stint, he fought in the siege of Yorktown, Williamsburg, Fair Oaks, Peach Orchard, Glendale, Malvern Hill, the Second Bull Run, Georgetown, Chantilly, Fredericksburg, the Cedars, Chancellorsville, Gettysburg, Wapping Heights, Auburn Heights, Kelly Ford, Locust Grove, Mine Run, the Wilderness, Todd's Tavern, Po River, Spottsylvania, North Anna, Tolopotomy, Cold Harbor, and Petersburg. By the time he was honorably discharged, he was a corporal.

After purchasing his hotel on December 14, 1875, Owen invested $5,000 in repairs and improvements. He even installed steam heat. Two wide porches graced the front of the building—one on the first floor and one on the second. On a warm summer night, a guest could relax outside in an easy chair before retiring to his finely furnished room. Sunday dinner could be taken in the dining room for 25¢. The bar, where cold beer was a staple, had its own ice storage room. Here Owen sold only the best liquors and finest cigars. After surviving so many perilous battles during the Civil War, Owen took pride in his establishment and in his customers' satisfaction.

Nathan H. Power, of the Power lineage, wrote about the village he knew in 1876. His article appeared in *The Farmington Enterprise* on March 2, 1933:

L.D. "Daff" Owen (c. 1885) was manager and owner of the Owen House from 1875 to 1898, after which his son Bruce took over. (Courtesy of the Farmington Community Library.)

> Farmington, at that time, was a village of wooden sidewalks, where there were dusty streets, frame dwellings heated by stoves and illuminated by tallow candles and lamps. There was only one brick dwelling in town. Grand River was a single track toll road over which farmers drew their produce to Detroit in strong heavy wagons. The roads were dirty, rough and at times well nigh impassable, because it was one continuous mud hole. About four hours was the time required for a farmer, with a good team and a load to drive from Farmington to Detroit. Four tollgates collected load toll from him in making the journey. The last one at Warren Avenue, where the streetcar line ended. There was no telegraph or telephone service.

That same year, a new town hall was built in the middle of Town Square on the northwest corner of Grand River and Farmington Road. Cynthia Collins, George Collins's widow, owned the property for which she received $800. Johnson Prall of Pontiac was hired to design and build the township hall, a two-story brick building measuring 30 by 60 feet and costing $4,300. The Masonic Lodge, established in 1868 with approximately 100 members, paid $1,150 of the total amount in return for a perpetual lease allowing them to meet on the second floor.

Pot-bellied stoves heated the building. Kerosene lamps blackened the ceilings. All major community events from plays to politics, to sports and graduations, were held here. The stately building symbolized the spirit of the city. Its very presence proved beyond any doubt that neither fire, illness, nor war could stop Farmington from moving forward.

The 1877 history of Oakland County describes the rebuilt city:

> Farmington village now contains three churches, the town hall, school building, one hotel, a market, three physicians—two allopathic and one homeopathic—one insurance agency, four general stores, one drugstore, one millinery and fancy-goods store, one hardware store and tin-shop, one shoe store and manufactory, two jewelers, one cabinet shop, two saddlery and harness shops, two shoe shops, three blacksmith and carriage ironing shops, two wagon shops, one foundry, one sawmill and one gristmill.

Farmington's three churches mentioned in the history were the First Baptist, the Methodist, and the Universalist.

After many years of service in Farmington's north end, the First Baptist Church relocated to its present site on Shiawassee and Farmington Roads. Cost for the construction of the new church ran $1,680. Now called the First Baptist Church of Farmington Village, the white frame building was opened on October 9, 1861 with Elder N. Eastwood presiding as first pastor. Fourteen years later, a new barn

The corner of Farmington Road and Grand River had wooden sidewalks (c. 1880s). To the right is the Owen House. (Courtesy of the Farmington Community Library.)

was built and a Sunday school library established. A new organ was purchased in 1876 and, four years later, a kitchen added. The building itself was shared with the Evangelical Society while they awaited the building of their own new church.

At the turn of the century, a decision was made to modernize the building. A vestry, connected to the main building by folding doors, was built along with a more modern kitchen. The original steeple was taken down and a larger one replaced it. With a new pulpit, pews, and carpet, the final cost for the renovation was $1,278. After being closed for four and a half months, the First Baptist Church of Farmington Village reopened in November 1900 with a special rededication ceremony.

The Methodist Church was another one of Farmington's earliest religious communities. Traveling preachers of the Methodist faith came to Farmington as early as 1825, holding their meetings in private homes—similar to most church services at the time. Finally Ebenezer Stewart donated land and, in 1840, construction began on a new church. It took four years and $3,000 to complete, but the little white church located on the corner of Shiawasse Road and Warner Street finally welcomed its congregation in 1844.

Services continued until 1878 when it became necessary to repair the building. Nathan Power described the church's reopening and rededication in several articles he wrote for *The Enterprise* in November 1929:

The First Baptist Church of Farmington is located at Farmington and Shiawassee Roads. The church has been here for more than 140 years. (Photo by Tim Ostrander.)

This portrait of Nathan H. Power (1860–1937) was taken in 1886. (Courtesy of the Farmington Community Library.)

> Dedication day came and it poured rain. The roads were deep in mud. Quite a large number of former pastors came in horse-drawn vehicles, the only method of transportation at that time. The speaker of the day was to be Bishop Ninde. He was coming from Detroit, about a four-hour drive. He was to preach at 10:30 and a large congregation awaited him. Never before had the church entertained a Bishop and there was a great desire to hear one so high in the councils of the Methodist body. Ten-thirty came, 11:00 came and no Bishop. Hymns were sung to while away the time. . . . Finally, the presiding Elder, J.M. Fuller . . . called the Reverend Thomas Stalker to the pulpit. Without any seeming embarrassment or hesitation he chose his text and preached a masterly sermon. I have always thought the Divine Spirit came directly to his aid for he seemed to touch the souls of his hearers and they gave him rapt attention. In the evening Bishop Ninde was there and preached. I, in common, with others, heard both sermons and I have always thought the one preached by Stalker, the most satisfying and inspiring.

The newly remodeled church continued in use until 1920 when fire destroyed it.

The Universalist Church traced its roots in Farmington back to Sergius P. Lyon, who built the Union Church in 1852. An interdenominational church, it attracted many members of the Quaker and Presbyterian religions. The Union Church was built near the Methodist Church, so near in fact, that the Univeralists owned part of the bell that rang in the Methodist Church tower. Each Sunday, the tolling bell summoned members of both faiths to their respective services.

Just before the turn of the century, the Union Church fell on hard times beginning with the death of its founder, Sergius P. Lyon. Without a permanent pastor, their savings reached an all-time low of $16.63. The church closed, but was eventually reopened by the Reverend C.P. Nash from Holly, Michigan. By the early 1900s, church finances were once again stable and a decision was made to remodel the building. Caleb J. Sprague, a trustee and vice president of the Farmington Exchange Bank (formerly the Warner Exchange Bank), took charge of the construction. With church members Carlos Steele, E.C. Sprague, B.C. Northrup, A.J. Crosby, and C.W. Button doing most of the work, the foundation was rebuilt, a vestibule raised, and a furnace installed, along with new pews and carpeting. The steeple was reconstructed and a new roof put on. The total cost for the renovation was $697.62. The building was rededicated on March 21, 1901.

A fourth church was built in 1892—St. Paul's Evangelical Lutheran Church. Thirty years before, German settlers came to Farmington. Members of the Evangelical Synod of North America, they organized the Immanuel Evangelical Lutheran Church in 1875. The members became divided and 23 men organized St. Paul's. They had no formal place of worship until Fred Gies sold the congregation a half-acre of land for $1 and, on August 21, 1892, the new church was dedicated.

The business face of Farmington also changed. It was no longer a frontier town that relied on mills for survival. With the forests now cleared, sawmills weren't needed. With improved transportation making it easier to take their goods to market, farmers grew less grain for the gristmills to grind. Their focus instead turned to fruit and dairy products. It took farsighted men like P. Dean Warner to reshape and guide the village into the twentieth century.

An influential businessman and persuasive politician, Warner was a man of the world. Taking along his 11-year old son Fred, he seized the opportunity to travel during our country's 1876 centennial. With railroads now connecting most of the nation, the Warner men visited Philadelphia to attend the Centennial Exhibition where, to public amazement, nineteenth-century technology was displayed. From there, father and son went on to Washington, D.C. They toured the Capitol Building, the Smithsonian Institute, and the White House where they even met President Ulysses S. Grant.

Two years later, Warner and son took to the high seas. This time, they boarded the U.S.S. *California* and sailed to Europe. They visited Fred's birthplace, Hickling, Nottinghamshire, and met the Maltbys, his biological family. After leaving England, they toured Amsterdam, Cologne, Strasbourg, and Paris. Theirs was a legendary trip that left the townsfolk back home in awe. The Warners were obviously a family set apart.

Despite his travels and public service, Warner still took care of business back home. He built a large brick building along Grand River in 1877 known as the Warner Block. The new structure housed a mercantile store and later a hardware store. When the village decided to establish their very own fairgrounds during the late 1870s, they chose the well-respected Warner as president of the Farmington Fair.

The Farmington Fair was organized just off the northeast corner of Farmington and Nine Mile Roads. For several years each fall, locals participated in annual baseball games and horse races while the First Baptist Church ran a dining hall. Special occasions were also observed there. The village held a spectacular celebration, complete with fireworks, at the Farmington Fairgrounds on July 4, 1881. That's when M. Byron Pierce drove a "high wheel sulky" and won the half-mile race in three heats. His time? 2:22, 2:21, and 2:20. Despite the excitement, interest in the fair eventually faded. After several years, the fairgrounds were closed and the buildings razed.

While local events captured the attention of Farmington's citizens, national news soon took precedence. The assassination of President Garfield hit hard. Like most communities, the people of Farmington were stunned and left to

The Farmington Baseball Team (c. 1895) often played at the fairgrounds. Pictured left to right are: Jim McGee, Bert Gates, unidentified, Clinton Wilbur, Fred Warner, Bruce Owen, T.H. McGee, Arthur Draper, George V. Conroy, Clinton McGee, and Harry Habermehl. (Courtesy of the Farmington Community Library.)

Edgar Rollin Bloomer was editor and founder of The Farmington Enterprise, *c. 1890. (Courtesy of the Farmington Community Library.)*

console each other during yet another hour of national darkness. Nathan Power remembered in an article he wrote for *The Enterprise* on September 26, 1929:

> Well does the writer of these lines remember September 18, 1881, the day of President Garfield's death. There was no telephone but the news had been received at Novi over the railroad wire and brought to Farmington by a messenger. It soon spread and a crowd gathered in front of the old [Collins's] store to express their sorrow. President Garfield had been a gallant soldier, had distinguished himself in the halls of Congress, was thought to be on the eve of a great career as president of the United States when he was ruthlessly shot down. The sorrow and indignation of the citizens was intense and they would have made short work of the assassin if they could have laid their hands upon him.

December 17, 1881 marked another important first in Farmington. An early library service began. Coordinated by local schoolteachers, books could be checked out for a two-week period every other Saturday between 3 p.m. and 8 p.m. Only one book per person was allowed with patrons being charged 5¢ a week for overdue books. The system worked well—it lasted for more than 30 years.

By the late 1800s, Farmington boasted blacksmiths, merchants, and a lone funeral director. In addition to apple orchards and dairies, cheese factories also sprang up and, in 1888, thanks to 33-year-old Edgar F. Bloomer (great uncle of former first lady Mrs. Betty Bloomer Ford), the village claimed its very own newspaper, *The Enterprise*. Bloomer originally ran the handmade newspaper from a small frame building that stood in one of his orchards. The first paper rolled off the press on November 2, 1888 as a young printer's devil, Fred L. Cook, pushed the ink roller across the face of the type between impressions.

That first issue consisted of five columns with a total of four pages. The front page carried the words "Independent in All Things—With Justice to All." The news reported was mostly of local interest—who was sick, who had been away, and who had visitors from out of town. Advertisements filled the front page touting hometown businesses. Sensationalism was also present as the main story of that first paper reported, "James Clark, a river man at Ludington, while maddened by drink, cut his mother's throat and she will probably die . . ."

A family affair, Bloomer's wife Lily took care of proofreading. Busy with her home and children, she had little time to spend at the office. An inventive man, Edgar would pin the papers under his son's coat and simply send the boy home

The Enterprise Building (c. 1887) is shown here with, left to right, an unidentified printer's devil, editor W.J. Richards, and Grace Temper. (Courtesy of the Farmington Community Library.)

to his mother. The entire Bloomer clan folded and delivered the four-page paper. Single copies sold for 2¢ apiece or a one-year subscription could be ordered for $1. In 1897, Bloomer moved the business from his orchard to downtown Farmington where he installed a modern steam engine to run the press.

Growing up with *The Enterprise* was another successful business, the Farmington Roller Mills Company. Located on State Street just west of Farmington Road, Louis Gildemeister opened the new flour mill, which competed for business with Sleepy Hollow's Pernambuco Mill, now owned by John Hardenbergh and known as the Hardenbergh Mill. Sleepy Hollow itself had grown. Besides the gristmill, there was a cooper's shop, a soap factory, a store, and a sawmill. Situated on the water, the gristmill was always a favorite gathering spot where locals could fish and swim in the summer, while winter months found them ice skating and sledding.

The beginning of the end for the Hardenbergh Mill came in 1888 when the main axle's shaft broke. Hardenbergh installed a new turbine waterwheel, but the modern equipment wouldn't cooperate with the old-fashioned machinery, hurting the ailing mill even more. Most customers took their business to the Farmington Roller Mills, which operated on steam, a more dependable method than waterpower. With the changing times, two flour mills were no longer needed and Hardenbergh was forced to sell his now inefficient mill while the contemporary Farmington Roller Mills prospered.

The Farmington Roller Mills is shown here from Farmington Road at State Street. (Courtesy of the Farmington Community Library.)

This image shows the inside of the Farmington Roller Mills, 1898. Pictured from right to left are Louis Gildemeister, his assistant James Adams, and son Leo J. Gildemeister. (Courtesy of the Farmington Community Library.)

By 1898, the downtown mill was running day and night, producing up to 50 barrels of flour every 24 hours. Farmers lined up with their wagons every Saturday morning. Their flour was sold to neighboring communities with one wagonful going to Northville alone. John Hardenbergh moved to Highland Park where he paid off his debts and made a new life. Hard of hearing, he was killed in 1919 by an electric streetcar on Woodward Avenue in the city of Birmingham where he was, apparently, picking flowers on the tracks.

The Gay Nineties saw even more growth in Farmington. James L. Hogle, a well-respected druggist and businessman, owned a drugstore. Besides medicine, he sold paints, stationery, cigars, and tobacco. L.W. Sowle owned a dry goods store, which he bought from John Collins. In addition to groceries and shoes, he carried crockery, glassware and lamps. A clever businessman, he enticed customers with bargain counters where select items could be bought for 5¢ or 10¢. Henry W. Lee, a harness maker, ran his business on the southwest corner of Farmington Road and Grand River. Known for his fine products, including

Henry Schroeder and his brother Herman (left) are shown here at their meat market, c. *1905. (Courtesy of the Farmington Community Library.)*

light and heavy harnesses, he also carried a full line of blankets and robes. Marie Gill was a milliner and dressmaker known for her fine hats and clothes. Her shop was a favorite among the local ladies. James W. Hatten owned a large equipment warehouse right on Grand River. Not only did he sell buggies, carriages, and wagons, he also repaired them.

Henry Schroeder and Jack Habermehl owned a meat market where the Civic Theater stands today. While customers shivered from the cold temperatures inside, meat hung on a rack along one wall and sawdust covered the floor. There were two rival blacksmiths, Thomas L. Irving, who was new to the village, and William Kennedy, who had lived and worked in Farmington for almost 30 years. With horses and stagecoaches as the main mode of transportation, neither blacksmith wanted for work. C.W. Chamberlin owned a barbershop where women weren't welcome. There he sold cigars and repaired watches. Besides being postmaster, E.C. Grace owned a dry goods and grocery store where he sold only the best domestic and foreign brands of hats, boots, and furniture, along with the groceries. He also offered the unique services of a dentist, Dr. Mason. Toting his foot-treadle drill, the good doctor stopped by on Fridays to care for customers' aching teeth.

As Farmington flourished, so did P. Dean Warner's son Fred. Enthralled by bicycles, the latest national craze, and fascinated by their speed, Fred began to race. Soon he was a bicycle champion, but when he paid $165 for a fashionable high wheel, he irritated his father, who considered it nothing more than frivolous. Fred proved the old man wrong when he opened a local agency. His bicycle business earned $800 the very first year.

Fred married Martha Davis in 1888. The young couple lost their first child, but had four more: Susan Edessa, Howard Maltby, Harley Davis, and Helen Rhoda. In addition to his hardware store, young Warner established the Farmington and Franklin Cheese Company in 1889. During its first year of business, the factory produced 40 tons of cheese. Eight years and 7,000 tons of milk later, production of cheese increased to 85 tons.

More cheese factories followed throughout Oakland, Huron, Clinton, and Ingham Counties. Together, they produced 1 million pounds of cheese each year. By 1905, production doubled with 90 percent of Warner's cheese being sold in Michigan and one customer living as far away as Scotland. Warner's cheese factories not only provided steady income to local dairy farmers, but offered steady employment to many others.

Farmington was also the headquarters for the Warner Dairy Company, which opened in 1892. A state-of-the art operation, local farmers delivered milk to the

Warner's Cheese Factory was on Grand River, c. 1890s. Most of the Cheese Warner produced was sold right in Michigan. (Courtesy of the Farmington Community Library.)

dairy where it was pasteurized before being distributed to thousands of customers throughout the Detroit area. Warner also built a cold storage building next to his house on Grand River where he stored fresh eggs and butter awaiting shipment. Along with his father, he also helped found Farmington's first financial institution, the Warner Exchange Bank, in 1898.

Warner joined his cousin C.W. Wilbur and employee Fred L. Cook to open a mercantile store. They carried dry goods, groceries, clothes, shoes, furniture, and dairy produce thanks to the cold storage building. It gave them an edge on the competition.

Fred L. Cook was born several months before the great fire in 1872. Shortly after his birth, Cook's mother died and his father moved to North Dakota, leaving his small son with Daniel and Bridget Lapham, Fred's maternal grandparents. As a youngster, Cook lived on the Lapham farm located on Nine Mile Road just west of Gill. After the death of his grandfather, Cook and his grandmother moved to the village in 1886 where they rented a house on Shiawassee Road near the First Baptist Church for $36 a year.

It was around that time that Fred Warner hired Cook to work in his store on Saturdays, where Wilbur was already employed. Warner paid Cook the handsome wage of $2.50 a month, but Cook, being an ambitious youngster, also took a job with Edgar Bloomer. He worked two nights a week as "printer's devil" inking

Clinton Wilbur, pictured here in 1898, was a cashier and one of the founders of the Farmington Exchange Bank, which later became the Farmington State Savings Bank. (Courtesy of the Farmington Community Library.)

Fred L. Cook, Farmington's long-term mercantile businessman, is pictured here at age 22 in 1894. (Courtesy of the Farmington Community Library.)

the old army press at the brand new *Farmington Enterprise*. Cook's job with the newspaper didn't last, but he remained an integral part of Farmington's mercantile business for over 50 years.

By 1894, Warner wanted to devote less time to the store and more time to his cheese factories and political life. Therefore, he formed a partnership with Wilbur and Cook. They called their business Wilbur-Cook & Company. Three years later, Wilbur withdrew to take on the position of cashier at the bank. He sold his interest in the store to Cook, who now called the business Warner and Cook.

Fred Warner took after his father. In addition to his shrewd business know-how, he was politically savvy. A member of the school board, he was voted in as president of the Village Council in 1891. It was a position he held for ten years while simultaneously serving two terms (1895–1896 and 1897–1898) as a state senator under Governor Hazen Pingree. At the time, Fred Warner was the youngest man to hold such a position, but he was just getting warmed up.

While Senator Warner served his country under President McKinley, the United States became embroiled in a brief war with Spain. In 1898, Spain ruled the island of Cuba, where several small revolts had occurred. Spanish soldiers herded the Cubans into detention camps in an attempt to maintain control. With minimal food and water, the prisoners gained worldwide sympathy. The United States sent its battleship, the U.S.S. *Maine*, to Havana Harbor on a peace mission

Harry McCracken is pictured here at age 17 in 1882. (Courtesy of the Farmington Community Library.)

hoping to give aid. Instead, the *Maine* was blown up and 266 men killed. The incident caused friction between the United States and Spain, which agreed to reform some of its policies in Cuba, but the Cubans wanted more. They wanted independence. When Congress declared war on Spain, Michigan was among the states called to military service. Five regiments of 1,000 men each were mustered. Among those that served were four from Farmington: Bruce Babcock, J.A. Welfare, James A. Wheeler, and Grant W. Wilkinson. It took only a few months to liberate Cuba and, by the year's end, most of the soldiers returned home.

Locally, that same year brought with it not only the Farmington Players, who performed at the town hall, but an educational accomplishment as well. The new Union School in downtown Farmington held its first graduation ceremony when three tuition-paying pupils finished the 11th grade. Well-wishers who came to witness the event filled town hall, which was lavishly decorated with the class colors of red, white, and blue. An evergreen arch bearing the class motto, "We Shall Reap as We Have Sown," was draped across the stage. Class valedictorian Maude Edwards gave a moving speech. The celebration ended with ice cream, strawberries, and cake, but not before Fred Cook presented Harry McCracken, Farmington's first school superintendent, with an Oxford Bible on behalf of the graduates.

Harry McCracken was born on July 14, 1865—the same day as Fred Warner. The two boys grew up together and remained lifelong friends. McCracken's father Charles came to Michigan from Burlington, Vermont in 1840. His great-grandfather Colonel Joseph McCracken lost an arm in the Revolutionary War while serving with the New York continental line. The McCrackens settled on a farm near Twelve Mile and Drake in Sleepy Hollow. After growing up on the farm and attending local schools, the young McCracken went to Indiana. There, he went to Valparaiso, a school for teachers. He returned to Farmington and took his first teaching job at the age of 17. By 1893, he became not only Farmington's first superintendent of schools, but the high school principle as well.

Built in 1883, the school itself was heated by stoves with long chimney pipes that allowed smoke to escape outside. When soot clogged the pipes, the ash would sometimes fill the classroom, leaving the teacher no choice but to dismiss the students. Occasionally, a prankster would put something ghastly, like red peppers, in the stove—another reason to send everyone home. Early curriculum consisted of "readers." When a pupil mastered the first one, they were allowed to go on to the second.

Diplomas were apparently controversial as the board of education felt they were a frivolous expense. When Miss Mercy J. Hayes, who claimed to be the first student to graduate from the Union School, completed her education, the board voted against buying her a diploma. The dilemma was ultimately resolved when a clever board member wrote to a diploma house requesting free samples. The delighted Miss Hayes then had her pick of several styles.

Nathan Power reminisced about his nineteenth-century school years in a speech he gave at the annual banquet of the Farmington High School alumni in 1925:

> School days! Who is there that cannot look back with pleasure to them? Filled with the happy memories of life's morning they are indeed precious to us. . . . Some incidents I well remember. An organ had been purchased for the use of the school. It would be too plain and cheap for the modern schoolroom, but to me it was a wonderful instrument capable of producing the sweetest music. Pupils were allowed to use it at recess and the noon hour if the selections were of the approved variety. One of the inflexible rules prohibited dance music.
>
> Most of the pupils brought their lunches and ate them in the school room at noon. Miss Wheelock [the teacher] and her two assistants went out for theirs. Some of the girls could play dance music and as soon as lunch was eaten one of the girls would play and others would dance. Pickets were placed where the teachers could be seen as soon as they appeared coming back from lunch. At the sight of them, the signal was given and either "Home Sweet Home" or "My Country 'Tis of Thee" greeted the teachers as they entered the room.
>
> One sad day, for some reason unknown, the lookout failed to give the warning and as the strains of "The Blue Danube Waltz" were most

The Class of 1891 are pictured here from left to right: (front row) Marinda Pierson, Perry Lamb, teacher Fred Lamb, Anna Thayer; (back row) Grace Thayer, Fred Cook, and Frank Steele. (Courtesy of the Farmington Community Library.)

> entrancing and a half dozen couples were tripping the light fantastic, the astonished Miss Wheelock walked in.
>
> Could a situation be worse or more horrible? The organ was closed with a bang, the bell rang and a solemn session of the school was held at once. The awful enormity of the offense was dwelt upon at length. Dancing and dance music in the sacred halls of learning! Such a manifestation of depravity could not be ignored. We were warned of what would follow a second offense and to make sure it would not occur again, the organ was locked up at the noon hour.

As the Spanish-American War was ending, changes were taking place across the face of the nation. New-fangled inventions were being developed at breakneck speed. One such revolutionary device that had people talking was the telephone. By the turn of the century, Farmington had its own telephone service as well. Making a phone call over 100 years ago was an amazing feat, but hardly convenient. The Michigan State Telephone Company set up pay stations in various Farmington stores. Would-be callers were forced to leave home if they wanted to ring someone up.

Things improved, however, as house phones were eventually installed. Telephone numbers, beginning with the number one, were assigned in the same order the requests were received. Despite the convenience, making a call wasn't easy. Static and other noise often made it hard to hear. Regardless of the drawbacks, Farmington's phones soon numbered 50. All were connected in the tin shop of Mike and Matilda Doherty, where the local exchange was housed. Night service meant that someone slept in the phone room.

Some folks referred to the revolutionary changes that occurred around 1900 as "progress," yet Farmington's ability to adapt ensured its place in the twentieth century. While electricity and indoor plumbing revolutionized life on the farm, the village welcomed a new church and the Detroit United Railroad (DUR). Once again, Farmington was in the right place at the right time. The DUR would thrust the tiny village full speed ahead into the next century. Suddenly, Farmington would have a whole new purpose and find itself a community at the crossroads.

Locals gathered to welcome the Detroit United Railroad from the south side of Grand River in downtown Farmington. (Courtesy of the Farmington Community Library.)

6. AT THE JUNCTION

The dawn of the new century was an exciting time of change throughout the entire country. Hints of horseless carriages, flying machines, and moving pictures fascinated the nation. Michigan in particular welcomed the revolutionary Ford Motor Company, along with the controversial Ty Cobb and the momentous arrival of the electric trolley. Booming with industry, Detroit celebrated its 200th birthday and found itself in the center of a burgeoning railroad. With more than 30 independent streetcar lines connecting the area, communities like Farmington were forever changed.

During the latter half of the nineteenth century, Detroit had a system of horse-drawn streetcars that began at Woodward and Jefferson, but horses could only go so far for so long. Enter local furniture maker Charles Van Depoele, who thought streetcars should run on electricity. He developed an experimental trolley that he took to Toronto, dazzling the citizenry there. Before long, he built an electric streetcar line in Windsor and, by the turn of the century, Detroit had several lines of its own. The trolleys operated on an overhead electrical system running on a track that was laid in the streets. The trains themselves were attached by a single wire to the electrical lines above.

Once again, Farmington found itself in the right place at the right time. The town's position on Grand River made it an ideal place for streetcars to travel. To the north were pristine lakes where city dwellers built summer homes designed for lazy weekends in the sun. To the west was the city of Lansing where the state of Michigan's government business was carried out. Rail travel through Farmington just made good sense, so it wasn't surprising when several streetcar companies came to the village with the hopes of laying tracks.

In 1899, after careful consideration, the Farmington Township Council chose the Detroit and Northwestern Railroad. The company wasted little time in laying its tracks, beginning at the junction of Orchard Lake Road and Grand River. The railroad, using gravel as ballast when laying track, built four separate legs making up the Orchard Lake Division. As a result, business boomed at the Farmington gravel pit. The pit, conveniently located just south of the village's business district, dried sand in a sand-drying house before shipping it out for use.

The southwest corner of Grand River and Farmington Road is shown here, c. 1910. The Henry W. Lee Harness Shop building still stands today. Behind the harness shop is the old Interurban station and behind that is the Farmington Enterprise Building. To the right is the Farmington Roller Mills. (Courtesy of the Farmington Community Library.)

Before long, Farmington Junction, where the four legs met at the intersection of Orchard Lake Road and Grand River, took root. The Grand River leg began in Detroit and continued west into downtown Farmington; the Orchard Lake leg turned northbound at Farmington Junction where it connected with the Pontiac and Sylvan Lake line heading toward West Bloomfield with a smaller third leg connecting to Pontiac. The fourth leg continued west on Grand River right through downtown Farmington before finally turning south at Farmington Road, where it stretched as far as Eight Mile and then headed west into Northville.

To support the new tracks and trains, the Detroit and Northwestern Railroad needed to build a powerhouse at Farmington Junction. To sweeten the pot and entice the township's approval, the railroad offered to supply the community with electric streetlights. The council agreed and the powerhouse, along with a 34,000-gallon wooden water tank, was built in 1899. Nine coal-fired boilers on the first floor powered eight generators with huge wheels on the second floor, producing enough power to run not just the trolleys, but also 25 street lamps positioned along the tracks throughout Farmington's business district. The council was very specific in its demands. Each light had to be 32 candlepower and burn from dark until 11 p.m. daily—except on Saturdays, when they would stay lit until midnight. The village would no longer be kept in the dark.

Not long after the powerhouse was built, Cleveland, Ohio's Everett-Moore Syndicate, headed by Henry Everett and Edward Moore, stepped in to consolidate the multiple railroads that crisscrossed Detroit. As a result, the Detroit United Railroad, better known as the DUR, was created. The Detroit and Northwestern Railroad was just one of the many lines bought out by the DUR.

Almost everything coming or going from Farmington rode the rails despite the fact that Farmington Junction had no station in those early days. There was simply a freight pickup on Farmington Road where the trolleys turned down Grand River. The freight shed and loading dock were always filled with milk cans and produce heading to market. At the same time, the DUR also delivered farming equipment, as well as goods to be sold in local stores. Before long, passengers were also part of the line and the freight trains were relegated to night travel. Farmington Junction eventually became a hub and, for the next 30 years, the DUR dominated the village.

A car barn was built on the north side of Grand River directly across the street from the powerhouse. All trolleys passing through the junction were required to stop at the barn for mandatory inspections. In addition to routine inspections, brakes were filled with air and repair work done. Behind the barn was a car wash and next to it a beautifully landscaped park for passengers to enjoy as they disembarked or waited for transfers. In case of bad weather, another building known as the waiting room provided shelter. Heated by a stove during the winter months, the waiting room housed several benches where passengers relaxed between their travels. Next to the waiting room was a small confectionary store

The Detroit United Railroad Powerhouse is shown here as it looks today from Grand River. (Photo by Tim Ostrander.)

This is a side view of the DUR Powerhouse. The old building is now home to several businesses. (Photo by Tim Ostrander.)

run by Charles and Sarah Barnhart. A favorite place among passengers and locals, the Barnharts were always good for fresh popcorn and peanuts.

The trolleys, used for both business and pleasure, ran daily every hour on the hour beginning at 6 a.m. They blew a horn or rang a bell to announce their arrival. For the first time, people from outlying areas like Farmington could work in Detroit. Likewise, people from Detroit had access to resort areas like Orchard Lake. For 10¢, many students also rode the line to Pontiac where they attended high school.

One of the most popular routes was the Triangular Trolley Trip. For under $1, site-seeing passengers could ride the rails from Detroit to Pontiac before transferring to Northville. From Northville, they boarded the Plymouth Division, which took them back to Detroit. The DUR brochure depicting the trip proclaimed, "This is the triangular route of scenic splendor through woods and meadows, over streams and along the shores of inland lakes—an electric ride among the farm lands and summer homes."

In addition to the passenger and freight cars, there were special cars. Mourners rented the all-black funeral car. Show goers rode the theater car for an evening in Detroit. It always returned promptly at 11 p.m.—except on opera night. The opera usually ran later and the theater car would simply wait. The work-car, nicknamed 'The Boat," carried lumber and coal. The Yolande, a parlor car complete with kitchen and wicker chairs, could be rented for parties. But the trolleys did more than just carry people and transport freight; the DUR also provided jobs as repairmen, conductors, and motormen for over 100 local men. At 27¢ an hour, paid in gold coin, the pay-car was enthusiastically greeted as it arrived in town each week.

The new trains also brought new risks. Accidents happened. Conductor Fred Stammann suffered a broken ankle when he attempted to jump from one of the cars. One year later, he suffered a more serious injury. *The Farmington Enterprise* described the incident on September 8, 1905:

> While engaged at his duties as conductor on a freight car of the Pontiac division Tuesday afternoon, Fred Stammann of this place was quite seriously hurt and although his recovery is expected, he is in a very critical condition at this writing.
>
> The accident occurred while the car was on the siding at North Farmington Junction and Mr. Stammann was standing on top of the car repairing the trolley when the fastenings of the trolley pole suddenly broke or slipped and the heavy iron fell, the wheel on the end striking Mr. Stammann on the back of the head and cutting a terrible gash and knocking him to the ground, badly bruising his shoulder and back. He was picked up and brought at once to the village where Dr. Holcomb dressed the wounds.

Despite the hazards, the DUR helped the community in a number of ways—ways they weren't even aware of. When A.E. MacKinnon, the new editor and publisher of *The Farmington Enterprise*, took over from Edgar Bloomer in 1899, the press was run by an old steam engine. One extremely cold winter, MacKinnon left Farmington for a few weeks. He returned to discover his steam engine frozen solid and cracked. A true newspaperman, *The Enterprise* editor firmly believed that the presses must turn no matter what. He quickly called a blacksmith for help. The blacksmith fitted a handle on to the steam engine and MacKinnon cranked out the next edition by hand. He recalled, "As long as I live, no one will ever convince me that *The Enterprise* did not have five million circulation that week."

Knowing full well he couldn't manually operate the press forever, MacKinnon devised what he thought would be a much better method. He rigged a treadmill to the press. He then talked "Hud" Wilcox, known for his fine horses, into loaning him a steed that could walk on the treadmill and at the same time turn the press. This worked well until the streetcar ran by. It spooked the horse, who frantically tried to run away. Worried about his horse's safety, Wilcox put an end to that venture. He took his horse home, leaving MacKinnon to think up another plan.

Luckily for MacKinnon, he had a friend who worked for the DUR. He thought MacKinnon should modernize his methods. He went to Detroit and bought a new electric motor, which they then hooked up to the trolley wires just outside the Enterprise Building. The only problem was the strong current, but the two men soon found a way to work around that; they simply placed a barrel of water outside the office and ran wires through it in order to decrease the voltage. MacKinnon ran the paper for two years before selling it to Harry N. McCracken, the school superintendent.

Along with the railroad, Farmington also welcomed the Salem United Church of Christ, built at the turn of the century. Reverend P. Malschat organized the first congregation in Clarenceville in 1875. Before that, most members were German and held early services in their homes. When Malschat arrived, he conducted German services in a schoolhouse every two weeks. By 1876, when a new church was built in Clarenceville, some members chose to worship at Farmington Village's new town hall. In 1901, the Reverend J. Bollens took charge of both congregations.

Later that year, the church bought a lot on Oakland Street from Fred Warner and construction began on the present-day Salem church. A building committee that included Louis Gildemeister oversaw the construction. On May 11, 1902 the cornerstone was laid. Inside it was placed church papers and records, along with the latest edition of *The Farmington Enterprise*. Five months later, at a total cost of $5,000, Reverend J. Bollens dedicated the new church. Services were conducted solely in German until 1929 when an English-speaking service began. By 1933, the German services stopped completely in favor of English.

While the Salem church opened, Warner, still a strong Republican, was serving as Michigan's secretary of state, but his biggest achievement came when he was

The Salem United Church of Christ, under construction in 1902, is shown here with its large bell in the foreground. (Courtesy of the Farmington Community Library.)

elected governor in 1904, during Teddy Roosevelt's presidency. Nominated unanimously as the Republican Party's candidate for governor on June 30, 1904, he defeated Woodbridge Ferris by 60,228 votes and served an unprecedented three terms. Destined for greatness and a source of pride to his hometown, Warner led not just Farmington, but the entire state of Michigan into the twentieth century.

As governor, Warner established the Highway Department, giving his support for road improvements. He also began the Public Domain Commission, which was responsible for the conservation of the state's natural resources. The commission later evolved into today's Department of Natural Resources. The railroads began paying property tax. With miles and miles of tracks throughout Michigan, this change greatly increased the state coffers, half of which went to the schools. Warner later supported a bill that lowered passenger fare from 3¢ a mile to 2¢. Besides battling the powerful railroads, Warner also supported the new primary election system, allowing the people to nominate the candidates instead of party officials. He favored prohibition and women's rights. During his administration, laws were passed to limit the working hours of children under 18 years of age to 10 per day with no more than 54 each week. Hiring children under the age of 14 in factories or stores was now against the law.

Warner and company are shown here on the campaign trail with father P. Dean in the back seat, c. 1904. (Courtesy of the Farmington Community Library.)

Governor Warner is shown in the governor's office in Lansing, c. *1906. Farmington's favorite son served an unprecedented three terms in office. (Courtesy of the Farmington Community Library.)*

Maybe it was his old friend's influence, but Harry McCracken, who had since returned to farming, became a member of the Michigan State Legislature, serving under Governor Warner. Part of their duties was to establish a state speed limit for the newly manufactured automobiles. Never having personally driven a car, McCracken visited a car dealer in Detroit where he conducted a study. After experimenting with various speeds, he returned to Lansing, advising lawmakers that 20 miles per hour was just too fast, but 15 would do nicely. Unable to convince his peers that 15 miles per hour was perfectly safe, the group voted in a more conservative speed—8 miles per hour.

In January 1909, the first fire company was organized under the leadership of Tom McGee. The men were divided into two groups—one, led by Fred Pauline, was in charge of chemicals, while the other, led by Amos Otis, maintained everything else, including the hook, ladder, and bucket brigade. In place of an alarm, a bell was mounted on a large livery barn that stood on Grand River. Whenever it rang summoning men to a fire, each man was expected to come with a pail in hand. Their first major challenge occurred six months later when a fire threatened the First Baptist Church. The organized fire brigade soon brought the flames under control, saving the church.

The year 1909 brought even more excitement to the village when Norbert Obright built a flying machine. He called it the Welch Aeroplane and even raced it against another plane at the State Fair that fall, causing a local sensation.

The Young People's Literary Union, c. 1900, were left to right: (front row) Clarence Utley, Myra Utley, Will Walters, Bertha Crosby, Myrtle Sowle, Floyd Nichols, Governor Drake; (middle row) Ed Moore, Suzy Severance, Perry Lamb, Emma Hinckley, Harry McCracken, Hattie Steele, Andrew Moore, Nona Drake, Mark Sowle; (back row) Arthur Greene, Ida Steele, Glen Power, Nell McCracken, Orion Everett, Frances Drake, Will Kyle, Enos Barber, Rosa Drake, Myra Green, Will Green, and Myrtle Smith. (Courtesy of the Farmington Community Library.)

By 1910, Farmington Village had about 600 residents. Most homes had a parlor where guests were received. Milkmen delivered milk in cans by horse and wagon. As they stopped at each house, they dipped out the allotted amount into a waiting pan and then quickly covered it in order to keep the flies out. Barns and farm animals dotted the countryside. Sometimes, the wandering livestock were troublesome. The Methodist Church ran a notice in *The Enterprise* that read, "The Official Board of the Methodist Church respectfully requests that no cows be pastured on church property."

Besides the Masonic Lodge and the Eastern Star, residents belonged to several social clubs, including the Epworth League, the Guild, and the Grand River Pedro Club. The Ladies' Literary Club met routinely for poetry readings followed by refreshments.

The library was another initiative that evolved under Governor Warner's leadership when the State of Michigan passed a law requiring each township and city to establish a public library. According to the State Constitution of 1835, local fines were supposed to be collected and used to fund libraries—something that was not being done in Farmington Township. When schoolteachers Martha M. Schroeder and A.J. Crosby pointed out this oversight to the Township Board in 1913, there was little they could do but agree. That year, a total of $2.11 was passed along to the library. The teachers then decided that it was impossible to be librarians and run the schools at the same time, so they promptly deposited their books at town hall.

The board appointed Martha Schroeder and the Ladies Literary Club to take over. They were given $600 with the stipulation that the money had to be shared with the cemetery—and the cemetery got first dibs. As a result, the ladies reorganized, calling themselves the Ladies Library Association. As the official group in charge, they manned the 800-book library on a volunteer basis and took on the responsibility of fundraising. They raised $140 that first year and rented out the Sunday school room from the First Baptist Church for a $12 annual fee. They purchased an additional 100 books and ended the year with $14.80 in their coffers. Hardworking women, the ladies also repaired and rebound worn books in their spare time.

Formal education in Farmington was also impressive. The *History of Oakland County Michigan*, published in 1912, gives a thumbnail sketch of the community's "up-to-date" school system:

> The school status of Farmington today . . . speaks well for the general advancement of the place. Today the school system of Farmington embraces a primary, intermediate, grammar and high school department, all of them being maintained in accordance with the most advanced ideas in educational methods. The primary department numbers fifty pupils; intermediate, forty; grammar, thirty-six and high school, forty-seven, making a total attendance of 173 pupils, with a corps of five teachers in charge. It is interesting to note that the high school attendance is almost as large as the primary enrollment—a pleasing circumstance in view of the general tendency to discontinue school with the grammar grades, so noticeable in certain districts.

Entertainment consisted of flamboyant characters, usually transients, who offered a variety of services. Fortune-telling gypsies wearing brightly colored clothes often came to town with their horses and wagons. Traveling medicine shows with their potions and elixirs promised miracles. Harley Walters remembered one in particular in an article he wrote for *The Enterprise* in February 1960:

> Medicine shows also attracted crowds. Each year at least one show would stop to do what it could for the health of the community. This writer remembers one practitioner who guaranteed his potent elixir would sustain anyone's life span to 100 years, including his own. He died that night in his wagon at Grand River and Farmington Road. He appeared to be not over fifty, but perhaps he had sold his last bottle and didn't have enough left to see him through the night.

The Nelson sisters, Hannah, Ida, and Eva, owned a combination bakery/ ice cream parlor on Grand River. In the front part of their store, they carried cupcakes, bread, and penny candy, while in back they sold dishes of ice cream for 5¢ or 10¢. If a customer felt like splurging, 15¢ could get them a large "Floating Island Sundae."

Bill Groves was now the town blacksmith. He normally charged 25¢ for a single horseshoe, but for the bargain price of 90¢, a lucky horse could get four brand new ones. D.K. Smith's Furniture Store was a two-story frame building located next to Doherty's tin shop. Deciding that home furnishings weren't enough, Smith expanded his business. He began selling Overland Automobiles. He ran an ad in *The Enterprise*: "Only pedals to push and no noise but the wind. That's the Overland for 1910."

Amos Otis owned the Farmington Lumber Company. His lumber and coal were brought directly to him by the DUR on "The Boat." Otis would then stock the lumber and deliver the coal directly to his customers so they could heat their homes. Wallace Hatton ran a woodworking shop. In addition to his business, he also built silos on many area farms. The Grace House was another of the village's hotels where public dances were held on the third floor. Frank White ran a grocery store that he heated with a potbellied stove in the winter. Most of his goods were shipped in wooden pails and, depending upon the season, he carried either fresh or dried fruits and vegetables.

Pool halls were frowned upon and generally considered troublesome places from where nothing good could possibly come. Nonetheless, Farmington had two—J.E. Phelps' Pool Parlor and William Walters' Pool Room. Both were favorite spots despite their unsavory reputations. Here men could converse about taxes and politics, as well as other relevant issues of the day, in between games of

Amos Otis's lumberyard was in downtown Farmington, c. 1890s. (Courtesy of the Farmington Community Library.)

The yard area of the Farmington Lumber Company is shown here, c. 1900. (Courtesy of the Farmington Community Library.)

pool. With no womenfolk to bother them, they happily chewed tobacco, smoked cigars, and munched on peanuts. Experienced pool players were even more privileged. They kept their personal cues locked up on a private rack. It was an honor not everyone achieved. Aside from the billiards business, Phelps also sold paints and brushes, while Walters offered his patrons a laundry service just to keep things on the up and up.

Inside the Warner Building were three businesses: McGee's Drugstore, Dickerson's Hardware, and Cook's Dry Goods and Grocery. Tom McGee's drugstore not only sold pills of all kinds, but also housed the post office where locals came to pick up their mail and catch up on village news. Day Dickerson sold pitchforks, horse collars, and lamp chimneys, while longstanding merchant Fred L. Cook carried a variety of items from underwear to cookies.

By 1910, there were approximately 16,000 cars in Michigan. Drivers paid $1.50 for a six-month license—no one dared drive during the harsh winter months. In Farmington, there were three such horseless carriages. Dr. Holcomb owned a Cartercar, Dr. Miller had a Buick, and the Warners had a wooden-bodied Jackson.

Electricity came to Farmington when the Eastern Michigan Edison Company built an electric line into the village. A controversial move at the time, the lights went on forevermore on October 28, 1911. Even the basketball team got into the act. Threatened with eviction for accidentally breaking one of the gas lamps at the town hall, Albert Bruder, their manager, personally wired the building so his team could keep playing there.

Now that the village had telephones and lights, its attention turned to the water supply. The village government approved $15,000 for a central water system complete with wooden pipes. To support the new system, a pump house was built and five wells were dug on Thomas Street. Water was discovered 138 feet later.

Three of the pumps were used until 1960 when Farmington finally tapped into the Detroit Water system.

The Botsford Inn, now run by Frank Botsford who took over after his father Milton died in 1883, remained a popular place. With the advent of the DUR, train tracks ran directly in front of the Botsford Inn for 30 years. As a result, travel habits changed. A trip to and from Detroit no longer required an overnight stay. In order to survive, the Botsford Inn had to change with the times. Instead of renting rooms, the inn played host to large groups and special events, achieving its first-rate reputation for dances and soirees. It was a favorite place among young couples that were courting. Here they could spend many a romantic evening listening to live music and dining on fine fare. One such young couple hailed from Dearborn; Henry Ford often brought his girlfriend Clara Bryant to the historic inn where they would "cut a rug."

Frank and Sarah Botsford, along with their two children Elizabeth and Owen, lived at the inn. In addition to his innkeeper's duties, Botsford also ran a receiving station for local dairy farmers who brought their milk to him. Botsford would then ship it to the Tower Creamery in Detroit via the DUR. Sarah Botsford often worked in the kitchen, cooking vast amounts of food for their guests. Elizabeth and Owen took the DUR from Clarenceville to Farmington where they attended high school.

Owen, a bright student, was a popular young man about town. He received a diploma from Farmington High School in 1901 where education at the time

An unidentified man is shown in front of Botsford Inn on Grand River, c. *1900. (Courtesy of the Farmington Community Library.)*

reached only the 11th grade. He commuted to Central High School in Detroit for one year where he completed the 12th grade. He then enrolled in the University of Michigan. Ultimately, Owen graduated from the U.S. Naval Academy at Annapolis in 1908. From there, he was stationed on the China Sea aboard the cruiser *Colorado*. Promoted to lieutenant, Owen Botsford was then given command of his own gunboat, the *Quiros*. He married Betty Calkins in San Francisco before shipping out. The young couple became a favorite among the Shanghai social set.

Then, while sailing on the Shanghai River in 1913, the unthinkable happened. The young lieutenant's charmed life ended because of what some say was poisoned water. Seven weeks later, the body of 28-year-old Owen St. Aubin Botsford came home. *The Enterprise* carried the story on August 28, 1913:

> The remains of Owen St. Aubin Botsford, who passed away about seven weeks ago at Shanghai, China, arrived in Detroit Sunday night, accompanied by his wife and the army quarter master general. Lieutenant Botsford was stricken while on duty on the gunboat *Quiros* in the Yang-tse River off Wusong and Hankow. Lieutenant Botsford was then commander of the gunboat, which had been ordered up the Yang-tse on account of the revolutionary trouble and to guard the interests of American citizens in troublesome districts.
>
> . . . The funeral was held from the home of his parents in Clarenceville Wednesday afternoon at two o'clock. . . . The body was guarded by U.S. marines and the casket, which was hidden beneath folds of the American flag was further banked with beautiful floral pieces. He was laid to rest in Oakwood cemetery and before his body was lowered to its last resting place his remains were given final military honors by a gun salute and the bugle.
>
> . . . Owen Botsford, who was a graduate of the class of 1901 of the Farmington high school, was the first graduate of the school to pass away and these classes number from the year 1890.

That same year, Fred Warner subdivided part of the family farm on Grand River. For $50 down, one of 70 lots located just south of Grand River could be purchased. Warner himself built the first two houses for employees of his cheese factory. A few years later, he built five more homes on Oakland Avenue directly behind the Warner Mansion. Some of Farmington's premier citizens, such as Fred Cook, were eager to buy one and move in.

But the village wasn't all business. Silent movies, a brand-new form of entertainment, were cutting edge. D.W. Griffith's *Birth of a Nation* took the country by storm. Fascinated by the magic of the silver screen, the locals, like most Americans, were amazed at the sight of moving pictures. In Farmington, the flickers were shown on a carbon-arc projector at the Methodist Community Hall. For 15¢ or 25¢, patrons could cry with little Mary Pickford, cheer for dashing Douglas Fairbanks, or laugh at the antics of Harold Lloyd.

The springhouse was originally built on the grounds by Palmer Sherman. (Photo by Tim Ostrander.)

The Farmington Silver Cornet Band, precursor to the present-day Farmington Community Band, made its debut in 1915 at the annual Decoration Day parade. Rehearsing twice a week at the waterworks hall, the band boasted 20 members. On coronets were Bert Gates, Clyde Price, Forest Pierson, Richard Marsh, Bateman Wood, Charles Sterman, Herman Grimmer, and Clarence Bell. George Robinson and S. Gates played trombone. On the tuba was J. Gates, while Henry Sallow, Frank Edwards, and Howard Stammann manned the drums. Band singers included tenor Garner Groves. Altos R.J. Auten, Charles Gravelin, Leo Hendryx and Stanley Gates rounded out with the lone baritone, Andrew Sallow. During the summer months, they played every Saturday night on the town hall lawn.

The year 1915 also brought Detroit lawyer Luman Goodenough to the village when he purchased a brick home on Farmington Road between Ten and Eleven Mile. Originally built in Victorian style by Palmer Sherman in 1869, the house consisted of a parlor, a dining room, and a kitchen with three bedrooms upstairs. Several barns, a springhouse, and a well were also on the grounds. At first, Goodenough intended to use the house as a summer home, but before long, he succumbed to the enchantment of his "Long Acres" and decided to make the home his permanent residence. He hired architect Marcus Burrowes to remodel the house. It was Burrowes who dramatically changed the outside appearance and turned the structure into an English country home with 20 rooms that included seven distinctly styled baths, a large greenhouse, and an elegantly paneled library. Outside were three porches, formal gardens, patios, pools, and terraces overlooking the breathtaking landscape of the farmlands. Goodenough also replaced Sherman's old picket fence with the stately stone wall that graces the front of the house today.

The Goodenoughs raised three children here. Out back, the doting father built a log playhouse for his children that still remains on the property. An avid gardener, he was known to rise at 5 a.m. just to work outdoors. Eventually, he hired several gardeners to maintain the lush grounds. Goodenough himself planted many of the trees still standing outside the house. Mrs. Goodenough died in 1967. Two years later, the house was donated to the township. Today, the elegant house is used as a community center where classes are held along with weddings and parties.

While the people of Farmington went about their daily business, international unrest was spreading throughout Europe. Soon, world events would escalate, bringing new challenges to our nation affecting every town and city between the Atlantic and Pacific—Farmington included. As in days past, the townsfolk rose to the occasion, accepting each challenge and bravely facing their own fears in a radically different world filled with lethal conflict. War, disease, and personal crisis, however, only served to strengthen and deepen the roots of Arthur Power's settlement. Maybe it was inborn, something inherited from those early settlers, or maybe it was just their sense of adventure. Whatever it was, the people of Farmington, despite the tough times, remained strong, celebrating their heritage and embracing the future.

This log cabin playhouse was built by Luman Goodenough for his children. (Photo by Tim Ostrander.)

7. From Village to City

While war raged halfway around the world, Ford cars sold for $325 and auto plants shaped Detroit. Farmington High School students studying physics were required to visit the auto factories, witnessing firsthand modern technology at its finest. Life in Farmington went on as usual among the dairy farms and orchards. The Halsteds sold apples while the Warners sold cheese. Before long, international matters would take precedence, but in 1915, Farmington the community concerned itself with local issues. New schools and curfews were in the spotlight.

That was the year when the village decided a new school, as well as a curfew, was in order. Attendance at the Union School was up to 172—more students than the old building could handle. Therefore, a $9,000 bond was overwhelmingly approved to fund a new school. The folks of Farmington wasted no time and, the following year, a brand-new all brick school opened at a cost of $14,000. Much to the students' delight, the new structure boasted indoor heating. The curfew, however, didn't fare as well. The schoolmaster, responsible for ringing the bell at 8:30 each night, gave up on the idea after only three months.

By 1917, the township's total value was assessed at $759,185 and our country found itself embroiled in another war—unlike any other that we had ever known. Although the fighting had been going on in Europe for quite some time, the United States threw her hat in the ring on April 6, 1917. Michigan responded to President Woodrow Wilson's call with well over 100,000 men, including all the boys slated to graduate from Farmington High School. Only girls attended commencements that year.

Among the young men who so enthusiastically enlisted was Harley Warner. He described his war adventures in the many letters he sent home. His parents, like other local families, shared their war correspondence with the rest of the town by publishing their son's letters in *The Enterprise*. On September 19, 1918, the newspaper carried one of Harley's letters that read in part:

> Have been stationed with the 135th Aero squadron for the last three weeks, a group of Armament officers which take in three other squadrons—these are the first four squadrons equipped in real American

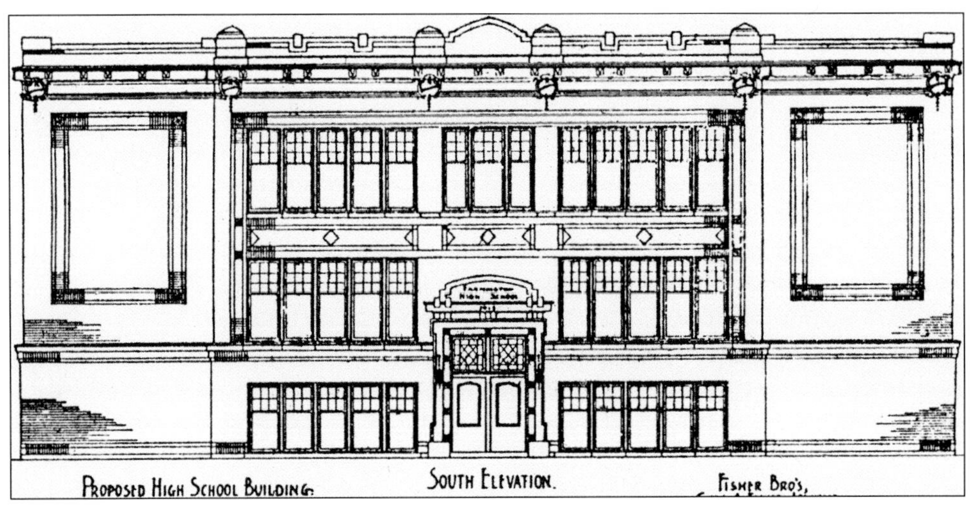

This image is a blueprint of the new Farmington High School, built in 1918. (Courtesy of the Farmington Community Library.)

> fashion, with Liberty Motors and they certainly are great planes. Have been up several times in them; once as high as 18,000 feet, and have gone as fast as 135 miles an hour, not at all bad, do you think?
>
> . . . At present we are located about six and seven miles from the lines, and have many exciting times—mostly during the dark hours of the night, but getting so I don't mind these bombing raids a bit—just trust to luck, and so far have made out very good.

He participated in 35 air raids and, before the war ended, Harley was in charge of the First Day Bombardment Group—the only United States bombing group that saw action. It was no wonder that Harley Warner returned home a war hero and was elected village clerk.

But four young men from Farmington never came back: Nineteen-year-old Bertrand Groves was killed in France on August 7, 1918 during the second battle of the Marne. Private Howard Eisenlord, who served with him, sent a letter to Grove's family describing the heroic young man:

> He was on patrol duty when he was hit, and he swam a river and walked a mile to the dressing station before he would let them fix him up. He had one arm nearly off and a number of body wounds. What put him out was the loss of blood in walking so far. He was a good fellow and there wasn't a better soldier in the whole outfit.

Farmington grieved. Flags flew at half-staff and businesses closed, while Groves was buried with full military honor. He was laid to rest by fellow members of his Company A, 125th Infantry, 63rd Brigade, 32nd Division, First Army Corps.

The following October, Lemuel Walker, a member of the machine gun company, 125th Infantry was also killed in France. High-spirited, the letters he wrote to his family were always optimistic and upbeat. Proud to serve his country, he often declared that being a soldier was his lifelong dream. Farmington's American Legion Post, the Groves-Walker Post 346, was named in honor of these two fine local heroes.

Farmington lost two other men during the Great War. Joseph Yerkes was Farmington's first casualty. Bert Middlewood died from Spanish Influenza at Florida's Camp Johnson, leaving behind a wife and six children.

Back home, the Michigan War Board appointed a committee for food preparedness. Fred Warner was among the members. It was the committee's responsibility to increase the food supply. To assist them, the federal government created new positions called agricultural agents and the committee was given instructions to fill these jobs. Farmington's own Harry McCracken became the country's very first agricultural agent. As such, McCracken collected all the literature he could from various farm colleges and passed it along to farmers to aid them in growing bigger and better crops. He was responsible for

The Graham family, c. 1900, are pictured from left to right: (front row) Mary Heliker, Sarah Grace; (middle row) Mr. Lockwood, Edith Graham, Sarah Lockwood, Ella Graham, Sarah Wilson, Ellen Graham, Gertie Graham; (back row) George Heliker, Will Graham, Jay Graham, Joseph Graham, Charles Graham, and John Grace. (Courtesy of the Farmington Community Library.)

working directly with the farmers, ensuring that as much food as possible was raised for the war effort.

War gardens sprouted up in vacant lots around the township. The first War Bond Rally was held on June 3 at the Owen House. Oakland County's quota was a whopping $1 million. In Farmington, the citizens surpassed their $40,000 goal by $4,000. Thirty local businessmen also joined forces to establish the Farmington War Relief Association. They gave the Farmington Red Cross $1,500 for supplies.

Fred Warner donated downtown office space where the Red Cross could meet and store materials. The ladies of Farmington were encouraged to stop in on Tuesday and Saturday afternoons. Here they picked up new material and dropped off items already completed in their smaller neighborhood sewing circles. By November, the ladies of the Red Cross proclaimed that they had made 3,000 bandages, along with 81 shirts and 65 surgical pajamas.

One such sewing circle met weekly at the Salem United Church of Christ in support of the boys at the front. The women sewed bandages and knitted socks and sweaters. They also sponsored bond drives, which were a rousing success, bringing in thousands of dollars. To show their allegiance, the church's congregation approved the following resolutions on June 30, 1918:

> To reaffirm our individual loyalty to this, our Nation and country.
>
> To express our sincere appreciation for the blessings of liberty which we enjoy as American citizens.
>
> That we subscribe to the democratic principles, which dictated our participation in the war.
>
> That we express our confidence in the righteousness of our aims as a goal of victory.
>
> That we pledge ourselves to make every sacrifice and perform every service to hasten the end of the war.

Afterward, a service flag with 14 stars was unfurled. Each star represented a serviceman from either the Salem church or the Clarenceville congregation who was called to duty.

Clyde Graham, lifelong Farmington resident, wrote about the war years in a booklet, *Memories of North Farmington*, prepared by the Farmington Hills Historical Commission:

> During the First World War rationing was quite severe especially on such things as sugar and fats but somehow Homer [Wolcott] was able to get sugar by the ton and sell it to his customers by the hundred pound bag for as I remember $33 dollars a bag. Farmers would take it and hide it in the oat bins. It was considered contraband by the government and if they were caught, it meant a jail term. Also at that time every family was required to buy Liberty Bonds according to your ability to pay (determined by a government survey as to your net worth). You

The old schoolhouse (c. 1905), built in 1888, served the community until it burned down in 1918. (Courtesy of the Farmington Community Library.)

> were not asked but it was demanded of you to do so to support the war effort and the penalty for not complying was tar and feathering. That happened in a couple of cases, no names mentioned, but they were people we knew.

Even the children were willing to do their part. They joined the Junior Red Cross organized by Oakland County teachers. The youth group staged variety shows and donated the admission charge to the war effort. When the Army declared that black walnuts made the best airplane propellers, the Farmington Boy Scouts searched the surrounding woods for black walnut trees. The enterprising young men found 115 trees for the cause.

When the war finally ended in 1919, Farmington could be proud. Consistently surpassing its war bond quotas, Farmington raised hundreds of thousands of dollars for the cause. The patriotic townsfolk survived rationing and a fuel shortage. They wholeheartedly gave their time and energy in support of the many Red Cross efforts. Most courageously of all, they sent 25 of their boys to faraway places, hoping that each one could make a difference in an unstable world.

As the nation recovered from the Great War and the automobile rose in popularity, paved streets took over where dirt roads left off. Talking pictures were all the rage. The radio brought a variety of entertainment, as well as breaking news, directly home. Prohibition left the country high and dry. Travel by air was reserved for the adventurous. The boys of summer captured the nation's fancy as locals cheered their hometown teams. Women demanded the right to vote. Closing in on their first 100 years, Farmington residents were proud of their rich heritage, but that alone hardly ensured their survival. They hovered between the old world of the settlers and a new world where rapid change overtook even the simplest aspects of daily life.

With more and more automobiles passing through, the first order of business after the war was the paving of Grand River. Prior to World War I, the dust stirred up by early cars was subdued with oil. Each summer, 5,000 gallons of the sticky stuff was applied to not only Grand River, but Farmington and Shiawassee Roads as well. With the oil shortage caused by the Great War, dusty roads became the norm. One year after the fighting finally ended, Farmington's main street was paved from the Junction at Orchard Lake through the downtown business section.

The old schoolhouse, constructed in 1888, burned down in 1918. The new school alone, now three years old, wasn't big enough to accommodate all of the students. Temporary classrooms were set up in the waterworks building on Grand River as plans were made for a new high school. A special election was held and taxpayers approved the bonds needed to build a state-of-the-art facility with a library, an auditorium, and two fully equipped chemistry and physics rooms. The new building opened on September 2, 1919 with 83 high school students in attendance. Longtime supporters of education, the local citizens were thrilled and showed their support ten days later at the open house.

By now, William M. Miller ran *The Enterprise*, an eight-page paper measuring 20 inches long with six columns. It sold for a nickel an issue, but for the bargain price of $1.50, avid readers received a one-year subscription. As the local paper grew, Fred Warner continued making news. After his third term as governor, he began a campaign to regain his senate seat. His run for office, however, lasted

Not much remained of the old schoolhouse after the 1918 fire. (Courtesy of the Farmington Community Library.)

only a week. Warner dropped out of the race after learning that auto mogul Henry Ford was running against him. Ford not only lost, but the whole ordeal turned him into a Democrat. Warner, still faithful to the Grand Old Party, went on to become Michigan's Republican National Committeeman.

Farmington continued to grow. Lionel Fendt started the Fendt Builders Supply, which is still in business at the same location. His grandmother Sophie Tamm came to Farmington from Fahrenholz, Germany with her family in 1868. She took a job at the Maple Cheese Factory on today's Gill Road near Nine Mile. In 1870, Sophie met and married Friedrich Fendt from Mechlenburg, Germany, who also found employment at the same cheese factory. In 1878, Friedrich bought the business. Five years later, the factory closed and the Fendts concentrated on farming. Members of the Salem church, they raised three children, the oldest of which they called Heinrich. When 52-year-old Friedrich died in 1893, Sophie continued running the family farm. Seven years later, Heinrich died suddenly on Christmas Day, leaving behind a wife and two-year-old son Lionel. His young widow remarried and moved to Livonia taking Lionel with her. In 1920, when a grown-up Lionel married Livonia's Elsie Rutenbar, he moved back to the farm on Gill Road where he opened the longstanding family business.

While Lionel Fendt was setting up shop, young Joe Himmelspach came to Farmington from Detroit. He bought John Lathrup's milk business, also on Gill Road. With the help of his horse and wagon, he delivered over 80 quarts of milk supplied by two local farmers every day. Bottle washing was done in laundry

The Methodist Church is shown here as it stands on Grand River today. Rebuilt after the 1920 fire, the church reopened two years later. (Photo by Tim Ostrander.)

The Children's Hospital is shown here in 1928. (Courtesy of the Walter P. Reuther Library, Wayne State University.)

tubs in the basement. Within two years, the Farmington Dairy expanded, forcing Himmelspach to move into a larger place—the old bank building on Grand River.

Churches were still an important part of rural life, promoting a sense of community. When the Methodist Church suffered a disastrous fire, *The Enterprise* reported it on February 7, 1920:

> About 9 o'clock James Hazelton passing, smelled smoke and discovered the fire, turning in the alarm, but before the department could get to work the flames had gained much headway there was no hope of saving the structure, and their attention was turned to other buildings in the vicinity, and the church edifice was a total loss, the only things saved being the piano, pulpit furniture and some chairs, some of which were badly scorched.
>
> We understand the building was insured for some $5,000 with about $500 on the community picture machine, the cost of which was in the neighborhood of $1,000.

Church members rallied to rebuild and a stately red brick building, rededicated on March 19, 1922, was erected on Grand River where it stands today. The new church's auditorium was the largest meeting place in the village and became a focal point for graduations, basketball games, and concerts over the next three decades. At the same time, the Methodist Children's Home of Michigan was built on Grand River west of Oakwood Cemetery. Sponsored by the Methodist Church, the orphanage took in needy children, but it wasn't the first institution dedicated to youngsters in the township.

The Michigan Hospital School for Crippled Children was originally built in 1907 east of Orchard Lake just south of Nine Mile. Detroit Mayor James Couzens made a generous offer in late 1921. He pledged $5 million if the Children's Free Hospital and the Farmington Hospital merged. The money would be used to erect a new facility for convalescent children. The hospitals agreed and the new facility cared for hundreds of children suffering from diseases such as polio well into the 1950s.

By 1922, Fred Warner was suffering from uremic poisoning. Against his doctor's advice, he hit the campaign trail with Congressman Patrick Kelley, his former lieutenant governor, now running for a senate seat. After the holidays, the Warners headed south to escape Farmington's harsh winter. While staying in Orlando, Florida, the governor's health declined. He was admitted to a sanitarium where he died on April 7, 1923 at the age of 58.

The state of Michigan and the rest of the nation mourned, but Warner's death hit Farmington hardest of all. An active participant in shaping his hometown, Fred Warner was a good neighbor, a trusted friend, and a generous employer. Funeral services took place at the governor's mansion on Grand River with hundreds of people coming from all over the nation to pay their respects. In between officials and dignitaries were local farmers, business associates, and schoolchildren. The *Detroit News* reported the following:

> In Farmington, it is Fred Warner, friend and neighbor, who is being laid to rest. . . . Farmington is proud of Governor Warner and of his achievements. . . . But the inhabitants will remember longest the boy who grew to manhood among them, the merchant and dairyman they respected, the neighbor they loved, the man every last one of them called Fred.
>
> . . . And although, the list of honorary pallbearers includes the names of many known throughout the state and nation, those who will actually bear the body to the grave are old friends and neighbors of fifty years standing.

A powerful local influence, Governor Warner was laid to rest in Farmington's Oakwood Cemetery alongside his parents P. Dean and Rhoda, and his great-grandparents Seth and Mary. Life in Farmington would go on, but the death of Fred Warner left a huge void in the village. No strangers to hardship, the people of Farmington once again proved themselves a resilient bunch.

That same spring, while still mourning the loss of their favorite son, the villagers gathered to plan a grand celebration. Farmington was about to have its 100th birthday. Hence, the Farmington Centennial Association was born. The group, led by Nathan Power, was responsible for planning the village's 100th birthday party the following year. In order to raise money for the affair, centennial buttons that read "Farmington 1824–1924" were sold for 50¢ each. Public meetings were held throughout the year and several committees were formed to plan each event from the parade to the horse show.

The first in a series of fundraisers began on March 7, 1924 when a banquet was held at the Methodist Church. Approximately 400 people, including some former residents of Farmington, filled the hall, which was decorated in red, white, and blue. As a reminder of the past, 100 candles were strategically placed on the tables. After dinner, guests listened to several speakers and singers. The program ended with a rousing rendition of "Auld Lang Syne" as everyone joined hands. It was a great way to kick off the hard work to come.

Two months later, another fundraiser was held. This time it was a costume ball thrown by the Farmington Women's Club. Residents dressed up as Quakers, Native Americans, and Egyptians, as well as white-wigged colonials. All agreed that their elegant minuet was the evening's highlight.

A log cabin, commemorating the founding of Farmington, was built near town hall. A replica of the original log cabins put up by the early pioneers, it had one room on the main floor and a loft on top that could only be reached by ladder. The citizenry donated all materials and labor. An iron box, containing a current issue of *The Enterprise*, along with a listing of township and village officers, was sealed within one of the walls.

A call went out to the locals for pioneer relics. Their overwhelming response yielded rifles, Native American artifacts, and pictures. Some offered spinning wheels and clocks, while others gave saddles and yokes. A register was provided for guests to sign. The cabin's most famous visitor, history buff Henry Ford, slipped in quietly, toured the cabin, and signed the guest book before leaving just

Governor Fred M. Warner died in 1923 at age 58. His grave is located at Oakwood Cemetery. (Photo by Tim Ostrander.)

A local lady rides her horse down Grand River in the Centennial Parade of 1924 with the Korner Barbershop seen in the background. (Courtesy of the Farmington Community Library.)

as inconspicuously as he came. Later that summer, the log cabin turned out to be one of the centennial celebration's big draws.

It all began on Thursday, June 19, with a town hall meeting. Encouraged to share their stories, no matter how insignificant, Farmington's oldest residents gathered together and reminisced about the old days. That evening, high school commencements took place. On Friday, various athletic activities were scheduled with the main event being a baseball game between Farmington and Milford. The team from Milford resoundingly trounced the hometown team on their very own turf.

A pageant depicting "The Making of Farmington" was planned for Friday night. Instead, a severe thunderstorm wreaked havoc, delaying the show until the next night. On Saturday, the Farmington Riding Club held its second annual horse show with 60 horses competing in several different events. A parade, led by the Romeo band, marched along Grand River. Elaborate floats and finely decorated automobiles vied for prizes much to the spectators' delight. A special "motion picture" was shown at the Methodist Community Hall where a large audience viewed hand-colored slides of many local historical spots. Despite Friday night's bad weather, the centennial celebration was an overwhelming success.

Farmington earned the right to celebrate. The community had come a long way in the last 100 years. From a fragile frontier town to a thriving village, the township not only survived, it prospered. Farms gave way to orchards and dairies, while train tracks and automobiles replaced wagon wheels and horseshoes. While Farmington took pride in their first 100 years, residents took the driver's seat and headed straight for the next 100 years—full speed ahead.

In the midst of centennial planning, auto czar Henry Ford bought the Botsford Inn. A history enthusiast, Ford and his wife had fond memories of the elegant inn and treasured its rich past. With the help of Frank Botsford, Ford renovated the old building and planted gardens on the grounds. He went so far as to interview members of the community and record their memories of the inn. The interviews are still on file in the Ford Archives.

A perfectionist, Ford demanded authenticity yet managed to incorporate modern conveniences such as city water. He restored the original kitchen, but added a newer, up-to-date kitchen. He even moved the inn back 300 feet to accommodate the widening of Grand River. Tea and sandwiches were routinely served throughout the day, but lunch and dinner were made by appointment only. High prices prevailed limiting patronage to the upper class. Henry Ford operated the inn until his death in 1947. The Anhut family purchased the Botsford Inn four years later after Ford's widow Clara died.

Normally a quiet town, Farmington also had its share of excitement. On November 19, 1924, the Great Farmington Bank Robbery took place. Four

This float, created for the Farmington Centennial Parade in 1924, was sponsored by the Salem United Church of Christ. From left to right are: (standing) Ruth Schroeder, Fred Maas, Helen Westfall Casey; (seated) Margaret Bollens Maas, Glen Warner, Emily Maas Sisson, Lewis Maas, Martha White Harms, and Gladys Landau Schroeder. (Courtesy of the Farmington Community Library.)

gun-toting bandits with scarves over their faces greeted bank teller Marguerite Moore at the Farmington State Savings Bank on the corner of Grand River and Farmington Road. Oddly enough, her neighbor Charlotte Walters called to warn her about the shady looking characters lurking just outside the bank. "I really didn't believe her," Moore recounted. "But sure enough, in walked the robbers." Quick-thinking Moore kicked a bag of money containing $3,700 out of view.

Bank president Howard Warner emerged from a meeting when he heard the ruckus. The gunmen wasted no time in knocking him out. The next day, the *Detroit Times* picked up the story:

> The bandits told all but Edgar Pierce to lie down behind the counter. They forced Pierce to open the vault. As Pierce and one of the robbers stepped behind the second door leading into the vault, it slammed behind them, locking them in. Another bandit attempted to unlock it but, in his haste, broke the key.
>
> The bandit with Pierce threatened to kill him if he did not get him out. . . . "Crawl over the top of the door," Pierce suggested. This the bandit did, ignoring $67,000 in Liberty bonds and taking, instead, $5,000 in non-negotiable bonds.

Then, as the *Detroit Free Press* reported that same day, the excitement began:

> Meantime, Dr. Frank Weaver, whose office is in the bank building with a window opening into the bank, hearing the commotion, looked out and saw that a holdup was in progress. He telephoned Sadie Cairns, the Farmington operator, who was in charge of the exchange at the time. The exchange is next door to the doctor's office, and also has a window opening into the bank. Miss Cairns verified the doctor's report by looking herself, and then began calling deputy sheriffs for help. She called Ben Myers, a barber across the street, who is a deputy sheriff. He dropped a razor with which he was shaving a customer, obtained his revolver and rushed into the street as the thugs left the bank. He was soon joined by H. Stammon, a grocer next door, who also had armed himself.
>
> . . . Seeing the men, the gunmen fired twice in their direction . . . Meyers and Stammon were joined then by Fred Clark, a farmer, and Forest Dickson, a hardware clerk, and the four kept up a fire at the sedan until it was out of range.

Before it was over, 60 cars with 200 armed men were on the lookout, but the robbers got away with the non-negotiable bonds and $9,500 in cash. Their get-away car, a stolen Cadillac, was found abandoned near Telegraph Road with an empty tank of gas. The windows were shot out and the interior blood stained. The perpetrators were never found and the money never recovered. It was something the villagers talked about for months.

Inside the Farmington State Savings Bank, c. *1925, located on Grand River and Farmington Road. The majestic building still graces the corner. (Courtesy of the Farmington Community Library.)*

By 1925, however, village residents had other things on their minds. They voted 72 to 8 in favor of turning Farmington into a fifth-class city with their very own city charter. A charter commission was formed. Members included Emory Hatton, Howard Warner, Clarence Bicking, John Fitzpatrick, Clinton Wilbur, Floyd Nichols, Wells Butterfield, Fred Cook, and Arthur Lamb. The proposed city charter was adopted on December 14, 1925 and Michigan's governor, Alex Groesbeck, approved it on January 7 the following year. A mayoral election was held and Wells Butterfield was voted in as mayor, winning over Howard Warner by only 15 votes. Farmington officially became a city. The City Commission of Farmington held its first meeting on March 1, 1926.

In the fall of 1926, former Farmington resident and schoolmate of Governor Warner, Francis Ernest Drake, paid the new city a visit. Drake left the United States in 1898 when the government sent him to Paris to act as the director of machinery and electricity for the 1900 World's Fair. He ended up living in Europe, taking positions with such companies as Westinghouse. When the war broke out, he became a lieutenant colonel and served as the chief of Control Bureau, Office of General Purchasing Agent. His honors included commanderir de la Legion d'Honneur, France, and officer Ordre de la Couronne, Belgique. Drake also organized and became the first commander of the American Legion in Paris. His stay in the city made local news as *The Farmington Enterprise* reported on September 25, 1926:

> Francis Ernest Drake, of Paris, has been visiting his old boyhood home at Farmington for several days. . . . Mr. Drake is the son of Francis Marion Drake, an early resident of Farmington, and is the brother of Mrs. Lillian Drake Avery of West Lawrence Street.
>
> . . . Mr. Drake was the guest of Mrs. Avery, Sunday and left yesterday on a business trip to Florida and Texas. This trip to America was Mr. Drake's ninety-eighth crossing of the Atlantic Ocean.

During his visit, Drake found his hometown still picturesque and, for the most part, a rural community despite its city status. Orchards and farmhouses blended into rolling hills and green pastures. With approximately 1,000 people living in the city and another 3,000 living in the surrounding township, Farmington remained one of southeastern Michigan's main dairy and fruit centers.

The downtown district continued to be a strong focal point where locals socialized and shopped. Toothbrushes sold for a quarter and a family-size tube of toothpaste went for 39¢. Cod liver oil, a household staple, cost a disturbing 75¢. Shoppers paid 58¢ for a dozen eggs, while a 16-ounce bottle of ketchup cost a mere 17¢. Moving pictures continued to play at the Methodist Community Hall. The 25¢ admission price held steady, but now film fans were treated to such sophisticated Hollywood fair as *The Unholy Three*, starring the master of disguise, Lon Chaney.

While the 1920s ushered in the Jazz Age, Americans found themselves listening to a new kind of music. It was an era defined by flappers, illegal liquor, and raccoon coats. Al Capone and John Dillenger made front-page news. Henry Ford revolutionized the workplace with the 40-hour workweek. Marathon dancing was the latest craze. Women were voting and the country was experiencing a postwar boom. Impressive buildings of amazing stature rose up in most major cities, but as the decade came to a close, financial turmoil took over where the good times left off. The country plunged into a disastrous depression followed by a second world war—even more devastating than the first. The citizens of Farmington took it all in stride. They hung on as their banks closed and their sons were once again called upon to serve their country halfway around the world.

8. Surviving the Great Depression and Another World War

As the Roaring Twenties turned into the 1930s, few suspected that all was not well. Nearby Detroit was quickly growing into its international reputation as "The Motor City." With automobiles becoming more and more popular, Farmington said goodbye to the DUR. Prohibition was repealed and the city opened its doors to a Canadian businessman who knew a good site for a winery when he saw one. Silent movies turned to sound and the downtown section hailed a new motion picture theater that not only boasted state-of-the-art equipment, but also air conditioning in the summer.

In just a few short years, things would dramatically change as the country found itself in financial despair. Farmington, like everywhere else, felt the pinch. Unrest once again spread throughout Europe as Adolf Hitler took charge. Then, as another war unfolded, the people of Farmington proved once more that their pioneer spirit was alive and well as they courageously faced one of our nation's darkest hours.

Before the hard times hit, however, there were good times. In 1927, Farmington welcomed its first Catholic church when Reverend E.J. O'Mahoney founded Our Lady of Sorrows. Father O'Mahoney held the first mass that September at "Villa Marillac," now known as the St. Vincent and Sarah Fisher Home on Twelve Mile and Inkster Roads. Two months later, a small chapel was built on the corner of Power and Shiawassee where the Ely farmhouse once stood. Here, where the present church is located today, Frances de Longpre was the first to be baptized.

Another Catholic institution, the Sarah Fisher Home, officially opened in 1928. Founded by the Sisters of Charity of St. Vincent de Paul, the group had been in the business of helping Detroit's sick and troubled children for years. The nuns opened the St. Vincent's Female Orphan Asylum in downtown Detroit in 1851. The sisters held an annual fair to raise money for the orphanage and graciously accepted donations. By 1882, several local Catholic groups sponsored the asylum and, by 1918, the Detroit Community Union pitched in.

In addition to the orphanage, the good sisters also opened Detroit's House of Providence in 1869 for unwed mothers and their children. Young mothers on their own were allowed to stay at the forward-thinking institution until they could provide for themselves. They also had the option of leaving their babies in the sisters' care. Children were kept at the House of Providence until they reached the age of five, after which they were transferred to St. Vincent's.

By 1920, more than 200 children were living at the House of Providence, which was now also serving the community as a hospital. Mixing that many children with sick people became a problem, so the Sisters of Charity obtained an 80-acre farm at Twelve Mile and Inkster Roads in Farmington Township. At first, the old farmhouse was used as a summer home for the children. By 1926, it became their permanent residence and was known as Villa Marillac. Two years later, tragedy struck as a late-night fire consumed the building killing one of the children. Thanks to the quick-thinking staff, the remaining 66 children were saved.

The children needed a home, so Charles Fisher, vice president of the General Motors Corporation, and his wife sponsored the rebuilding. Renamed the Sarah Fisher Home after their benefactors' daughter, the new institution accommodated 240 children. *The Enterprise* described the new $1-million facility on November 28, 1929:

> Ten cottages, a two-story administration building and a chapel, playroom, infirmary, dining rooms, and nursery rooms have replaced

The sisters of Charles Ely—with the exception of his niece, seated on the porch— are shown here, c. 1900. Pictured from left to right are: Sarah Lapham, Martha Hatton, Mary Hatton (Martha's daughter), Minnie Paulger, and Jessie Meyers. (Courtesy of the Farmington Community Library.)

> the old single structure that burned to the ground on November 26, 1928. Located on 80 acres of rolling ground, with a stream running along the west side, the new home provides natural surroundings such as few children can enjoy.

While the Sarah Fisher Home was planning its grand opening, most Americans—Farmington residents included—were enjoying an unprecedented time of prosperity. An honest man, if he didn't farm, could find an honest job. Modern conveniences such as refrigerators and washing machines were available at reasonable prices. A brand-new Pontiac could be bought for less than $800. No cash? No problem. Getting a loan was easy. Air travel was on the rise. Before long, anyone could fly across the country—from New York to Los Angeles—in 24 hours, minus the overnight stop in Kansas City. Life was never better as the general population looked forward to a secure future. The financial state of the country was the last thing on most people's minds.

In 1929, Farmington was more concerned with the death of Mrs. W.H.H. Smith, wife of Farmington's last Civil War veteran. Coffee was 45¢ per pound. Henry Wadenstorer and his son Frazer were now running the Steele Mill. Along with the flour and feed mill, they incorporated a cider mill. For most folks, life on the farm went on as usual with no inkling of the bleak years to come.

Then, in October 1929, the bottom fell out as the stock market plummeted. At first, it seemed a distant problem. Something that happened as far away as New York couldn't possibly affect the State of Michigan—especially the peaceful farms and orchards of Farmington. Even the suicide of 37-year-old banker Clarence Chafy in nearby Walled Lake one year later shed little light on the seriousness of the situation. *The Enterprise* reported Chafy's death on September 25, 1930:

> Residents of Walled Lake and vicinity, dazed beyond expression by the suicide Wednesday afternoon of Clarence Chafy, cashier of the Peoples Bank of Walled Lake, are speculating upon possibilities arising from reports that difficulties with the Federal Reserve System in Detroit might have had something to do with the suicide.
>
> . . . Nothing definite that would indicate the immediate cause of the suicide has been found. Friends believe that Mr. Chafy, rather than planning to end his life, may have committed suicide on a momentary impulse, picking up the revolver that was kept in the bank vault for protection.
>
> . . . Mr. Chafy was found dead in the vault by his wife . . . [He] had shot himself through the heart with the bank's .32 Caliber pistol.

Farmington had more immediate matters to face and the state of the economy wasn't one of them. After 30 years of service, the DUR closed down, giving way to the more convenient automobile. It was a blow to the city that depended on the trolleys for jobs, transportation, and commerce, but life went on. Joe Himmelspach moved his Farmington Dairy into the newly remodeled Farmington train depot. Before long, another business offering new jobs and opportunities settled into the neighborhood.

Canadian businessman Morris Twoney had his eye on Farmington Junction. Twoney, founder of the Windsor Wine Company in Walkerville, Ontario, had a plan. Once the United States Congress repealed prohibition, Twoney left Canada for the United States. He came to Farmington and established LaSalle Wines and Champagne, Inc. on April 10, 1933, moving into the old DUR Powerhouse at the junction on Grand River. Twoney went to work remodeling the 83,000-square-foot building. He lowered the ground floor and installed large oak aging casks. Fermenting vats were put in on the second floor. He also added a third floor to house crushing vats, while offices were set up in the front section of the ivy-covered building.

Using only Michigan grapes, LaSalle soon gained its sparkling reputation. From the Blue Concord grape came dark wines. The Niagara, a yellowish-gold grape, was used for white wines, and the rose-colored Delaware grape yielded sherries. After the grapes were crushed, the juice was kept in 20 glass-lined fermentation tanks where the sugar naturally turned into alcohol. Each tank held approximately 6,000 gallons. Once the wine was ready, it was pumped from the fermentation

LaSalle Wines and Champagne, Inc. is shown here as it stood on Grand River in 1935. (Courtesy of the Walter P. Reuther Library, Wayne State University.)

This Windsor Club label is from the LaSalle Winery. (Courtesy of the Farmington Community Library.)

tanks into storage tanks while waiting to be bottled. By 1939, Twoney added a new automated bottling room, making LaSalle the first winery in Michigan to have such contemporary equipment.

When transporting wine throughout the state became an issue, Twoney established warehouses in Flint, Grand Rapids, Battle Creek, and Marquette. He then stocked each one with a complete line of wines. Every warehouse maintained its own regiment of sleek LaSalle trucks, ensuring that deliveries could be made throughout the state in a matter of hours. As a result, LaSalle became one of the top-selling wineries, not only in Michigan, but across the country, successfully competing with even the finest California wines.

While Morris Twoney set up shop, Farmington welcomed home another distinguished citizen of the world, Sergius P. Grace. Grace was born in the village of Farmington on October 11, 1875. As a youth, he told his father that he wanted to be a doctor. His father abruptly advised him to study electricity instead. Grace did as he was told and graduated from the University of Michigan's department of electrical engineering in 1896. He took a job at the new cutting-edge telephone company and soon gained attention with his work in preventing erosion of underground cables.

By the time he returned to Farmington in 1932, he had attained the position of assistant vice president of the Bell Telephone Laboratories in New York, as well as president of the New York Electrical Society. His innovative work in communications and electrical science created a stir and before long he joined the lecture circuit. Just before Grace returned to Farmington, he received two honorary doctorate degrees—one from the University of Michigan and one from Notre Dame. An enthusiastic crowd welcomed Dr. Grace home as *The Enterprise* reported on June 23, 1932:

> In his public appearances the last few years, he has done much to bring about a clearer understanding of the research and development work that has made possible today's world-wide telephone system and its by-products, such as the telephotograph, television, teletypewriter, artificial larynx, hearing aids for the deaf, talking motion pictures and orthophonic phonograph. He has helped greatly to popularize the work of the scientist and to bridge the gulf between science and business.
>
> . . . He seemed genuinely astonished when, as he was presented by the toastmaster, his audience rose as one to honor and applaud him; again when the program was over he could not leave without rising again to thank the people of his birthplace for their homage. One hopes that despite his modesty, he gained in those few hours an understanding of the pride with which Farmington claims him as its own.

Despite the local excitement and the good work of people like Dr. Grace, the national economic picture wasn't bright. Unemployment rates rose during the 1930s and confidence in the state of the economy dropped. A nationwide panic ensued. Although Farmington felt the aftermath of job loss and bread lines, the city itself and the surrounding township did not rely on big business to survive. Instead local farmers found creative ways to offset their financial losses. Take Joseph Gravlin, for instance. He opened a food stand right on his farm during those rough years. Located at Northwestern Highway and Thirteen Mile Road, fresh produce was sold there every weekend until 1985 when the stand closed for good.

The city's two banks, however, were a different story. Much like other banks of the time, the Farmington banks were experiencing financial turmoil. Both the Peoples State Bank and the Farmington State Savings Bank were among the Michigan financial institutions forced to close on February 14, 1933 by order of Governor William Comstock. He declared a statewide "bank holiday," thereby closing all of Michigan's financial establishments, affecting a total of 436 banks and trust companies and freezing $1.5 billion. Michigan was the first state in the nation to take such drastic action, but other states soon followed. Within three weeks, only a handful of states were left with banks still open for business.

The newly elected president, Franklin Delano Roosevelt, was forced to declare a nationwide bank holiday, closing the rest. Before they even knew what happened, people were left with only the money in their pockets. Stunned by such extreme measures, Farmington's citizens, much like the rest of the nation, stayed home to hear the first of Roosevelt's famous "fireside chats" broadcast over the radio waves on March 12, 1933.

It was hardly what P. Dean Warner had in mind when he began helping his neighbors, well before the turn of the century. As Farmington's first, albeit unofficial, banker, Warner not only loaned the locals money, but took care of their other financial matters as well. His informal position made way for the Warner Exchange Bank, which grew into the Farmington Exchange Bank. In 1898, the financial institution moved into a new brick building on Grand River just east of Farmington Road. Beginning with a modest $100,000 in financial backing, Warner became president, C.J. Sprague vice president, and C.W. Wilbur cashier. The only one of its kind in the township, the bank prospered.

By 1910, the Farmington Exchange Bank was reorganized into a state bank with Fred Warner as president and assets worth approximately $150,000. It turned into one of Oakland County's most significant banks so it was no surprise when, in 1916, an attempted robbery occurred. A 2-foot-square hole was cut in the roof directly over the vault. What the robbers didn't count on was the thick, impenetrable wall surrounding the vault. Discouraged, they left the premises without a dime.

The following year, the Farmington Exchange Bank changed its name to the Farmington State Savings Bank. At the same time, competition was close on its heels. The Peoples State Bank-Farmington also opened for business on Grand River. Pharmacist James L. Hogle was president with Benjamin E. Storms cashier, and Charles H. Ely and William Maas, directors.

This two-story building, which formerly housed the Peoples State Bank, stands on Grand River today. (Photo by Tim Ostrander.)

This image shows a view of Grand River and the Peoples State Bank looking west, c. 1930. (Courtesy of the Farmington Community Library.)

Both vying for local customers, each bank erected a large building on Grand River. The Peoples State Bank announced a renovation of its facility, located on the north side of Grand River between two Doric columns. At the same time, the Owen House was moved back to make way for the new business block that would be home to the Farmington State Savings Bank. The Farmington Improvement Association, also stockholders of the bank, built the imposing structure directly on the corner of Grand River and Farmington Road. The new bank building also housed a basement restaurant, eight first-floor businesses, and second-floor apartments. At the center of the building with its grand entranceway was none other than the Farmington State Savings Bank. Eventually, Fred Warner's son Howard took over as president.

In the throes of the Great Depression, the Peoples State Bank gave way to financial stress and eventually became part of the Detroit Bank & Trust (now Comerica Bank), while the Farmington State Savings Bank was able to reopen as the Farmington State Bank on May 19, 1934. A grand celebration was planned to hail what everyone considered a major accomplishment. *The Enterprise* was once again on the job as it reported the news on May 3, 1934:

> Plans are being carried forward for the community celebration which is to mark the opening of the bank two weeks hence. With setting of the date accomplished, genuine activity is expected to begin within a

> few days to make May 19 one of the outstanding days in Farmington's history . . . and it is anticipated that the results will provide residents of not only Farmington but the neighboring territory with an event that will long be remembered.

The program started at 7:30 a.m. as free raffle tickets were distributed for prizes donated by Farmington businesses. At nine, the bank officially opened with Mrs. Perrin Glidden establishing the first commercial account. That afternoon, an Apple Blossom Tour began on Grand River winding throughout the area. The Drum and Bugle Corps of Detroit Edison's Post No. 187 provided entertainment. A special dinner was served at the Methodist Church later in the evening, followed by a dance marking the end of a day filled with excitement, as well as a sense of accomplishment.

There was even a song written by Farmington's own poet Marie Walling to commemorate the event. Written to the tune of "When It's Apple Blossom Time in Normandy," Walling called her version "When It's Apple Blossom Time in Farmington."

Years later, the Farmington State Bank sold out to the National Bank of Detroit (NBD). NBD built its own much smaller facility on Farmington Road just south of State Street. The majestic downtown building is now home to the Village Mall. The only remnants of the original bank are the "FSB" initials at the top of the building and the now-sealed deposit box in the sidewall. NBD has since sold out to First Bank, which remains today in the smaller bank building.

Overall, the Great Depression affected Farmington much like it did the rest of the nation. When the hard times hit, Farmington was on the verge of transitioning from a rural community into an integral part of urban Detroit. Development was delayed, however, when the country hit the financial skids. Then came World War II, causing a shortage of construction materials and placing the city's growth on temporary hold.

By 1936, Hitler was sending his troops to the Rhineland and ordering German armed forces to the French border—a direct violation of the treaty that ended World War I. That same year, Frazer Wadenstorer dismantled the old Steele Mill and sold the cider-making parts to the Tibbits Mill, located near the Sarah Fisher Home. Wadenstorer then turned his property into a fruit farm, where he worked part time in between construction jobs. This wasn't unusual. By now, most local farmers worked a job outside the farm to make ends meet.

Overseas, events continued to escalate as Hitler and his army advanced across Europe. In 1939, the Germans invaded Prague before entering Poland, officially marking the start of World War II. By 1940, Italy entered the war and France signed an armistice with Germany. On the home front, international events were generally frowned upon, but actually entering into a war was not yet an option. President Roosevelt was elected to a third term in office. Car production in Michigan was finally on the rise after suffering through the Depression's leanest years. Farmington, with less than 2,000 households, recorded an official population of 1,510, while the surrounding township boasted 5,695 and its very own airport.

Kris Port, a 140-acre airport, was originally established on the west side of Orchard Lake just south of Thirteen Mile Road in 1936. Chris Kristiansen, who hoped to boost local economy with an air freight service, built his airfield with two runways, each measuring 200 feet in width and approximately 2,000 feet in length. An entrepreneur, Kristiansen also sold aircraft on the premises and, amazingly, Kris Port became a busy place.

Some might think it was an odd spot for an airport, but two Royal Canadian pilots would disagree. Forced into an emergency landing during a storm in the late 1930s, they were glad to see it. So glad, in fact, they proudly displayed their fighter planes to local residents before once again taking off for the friendly skies.

Michigan Governor G. Mennen Williams often used Kris Port for official landings when visiting the Detroit area. Some of the more venturous local residents took flying lessons there. Eventually, Kris Port closed and the Woodbrook subdivision was built over the runways.

As a new decade began, motion pictures remained a popular and inexpensive form of entertainment. They provided a brief escape from daily struggles. Movie fans laughed at the antics of James Stewart, Cary Grant, and Katharine Hepburn in *The Philadelphia Story*. They also took a good, somber look at themselves as they watched Henry Fonda in *The Grapes of Wrath*.

Millions of people flocked to their local theaters throughout the Depression, but movies weren't the only enticement. Theaters offered bonuses. Cash drawings were held on bank nights. Free dishes or silverware were often given away. Sometimes, on a hot summer day, patrons were lured inside simply for the air conditioning. It was an entertaining, not to mention inexpensive, way to beat the heat.

Lucky for Farmington, Edward Hohler loved the movies. Originally from Adrian, Michigan, 12-year-old Hohler got his first job at the Family Theater where silent movies played. He rang a gong. Once Hohler graduated from high school, he took over as manager. From there, he managed several local theaters and, in 1938, he took a job with Associated Theatres. Now, living in Walled Lake, Hohler's daily drive to The Granada at West Warren and Junction on Detroit's west side took him along Grand River right through the heart of downtown Farmington. Hohler knew his business and when he deemed Farmington a perfect place for a new movie theater, his superiors agreed.

The site of an old grocery store that stood directly on Grand River was selected and the two-story frame building torn down. Architect Howard C. Crane, designer of Detroit's elegant Fox Theater, was hired to plan Farmington's new movie house. Construction began in 1939. Hohler was named manager and with a Hollywood-style grand opening, the 700-seat theater was unveiled the following year. Sponsored by the Farmington Exchange Club and hosted by club president Dr. Lee Halsted, a formal dinner was held at Huck's Redford Inn, located at Seven Mile and Grand River. Afterward, the party moved to the Civic Theater

Dr. Lee Halsted (c. 1990) was Farmington's family doctor for almost 50 years. (Courtesy of the Farmington Community Library.)

where a special showing of *The Hired Wife* took place. That night, attendees were asked to sign a board dedicated to the new theater. The board itself still hangs in the theater today.

The Farmington Enterprise touted the Civic's opening on September 19, 1940:

> You'll open your eyes, when we open our doors. You'll find a new type seat, roomier, softer, more comfortable than any theatre seat you ever sat in. You can stretch and relax to your heart's content. And it will be cool, regardless of what the weather conditions may be outside. . . . No expense was to be spared to bring you the coolest comfort on the hottest day. Perfect visibility on the new, large silver screen, with perfect sound from the very newest super-sensitive sound equipment and scientifically tested acoustics will guarantee your enjoyment of the fine programs offered. Any seat you may select will offer you easy vision. All these plus beautiful surroundings, refined, clean atmosphere, courteous service, cool comfort, soft seats, make the CIVIC THEATRE, in Farmington, a show place fit for a king.

While the Civic Theater opened to the public, Congress was busy establishing a military draft in an effort to expand the armed forces. Blissfully unaware of the violent times ahead, the people of Farmington delighted in their new state-of-the-art theater. Patrons could always count on seeing a double feature, along with a cartoon or short comedy for a slim admission price—a quarter for adults or a dime for children—plus a 3¢ sales tax. With its oversized marquee, the Civic Theater dramatically changed the face of downtown Farmington forever.

As popular as the movies were, listening to the radio remained another favorite pastime. *The Lone Ranger* with its western flair had long been one of radio's most listened-to programs. Traveling on his white horse Silver, the masked crusader was a hero of epic proportions. He and his companion Tonto became legendary as they fought for justice. Actor Earle Graser took the starring role in 1933, becoming a national sensation best known for his trademark line: "Hi Yo Silver! Away!"

For the residents of Farmington, it wasn't unusual to see the Lone Ranger riding his horse around town. Graser and his wife Jeane bought the Botsford House near Ten Mile Road, settling there at the peak of his fame. Unfortunately,

Farmington's Civic Theater is a well-known local landmark. Its marquee has been part of the downtown district for over 60 years. (Photo by Tim Ostrander.)

their happy times didn't last long. Graser's career and life were cut short as he drove home from Detroit early one morning in 1941. Apparently, he fell asleep at the wheel. His car struck a trailer truck parked in front of the Methodist Church on Grand River. Graser died in the accident, leaving the city saddened and making way for Brace Beemer, who went on to become the most famous Lone Ranger of all.

As 1941 drew to a close, the Japanese bombed Pearl Harbor on the peaceful Hawaiian island of Oahu, stunning the nation. It was a defining moment not only in the war, but in the heart of each American. Four days later, *The Farmington Enterprise* carried a message to its readers:

> Although Farmington is far from the field of war action, its people are kept constantly on their toes by the apparent daring and aggressiveness thus far shown by the forces of Japan. As a solid part of this the United States, Farmington is at war. It has a big job to do, one of supplying its country with the resources present here.
>
> These resources take many different forms. The first and most important, from a material standpoint is to bend all our efforts in producing war supplies created in our community. We must produce and build with more speed and accuracy than has ever been known by the human race.
>
> Financially Farmington's job will be to produce as much as possible in assistance to the United States through investments in its country. This means considerable sacrifice on the part of each individual in order to see the United States and the democratic way of life victorious.
>
> The extreme importance of strong naval forces can not be over emphasized. . . . The United States has now been attacked and every man eligible for service should volunteer.
>
> The most important job Farmington has is to develop a sincere desire to see this war through to final victory. We must be steadfast in our determination to win even though it means great sacrifice on the part of all of us.
>
> All of these jobs begin in Farmington and it is right here that the Japanese will find a wall they can not climb.

The residents of Farmington took each job seriously. A Defense Council was formed under the leadership of Mayor Leo Gildemeister. The group, responsible for organizing all war-related activities, split itself into six divisions. Harold Oldenburg was named head of the Fire Division and in charge of putting out all fires, as well as maintaining fire and air raid alarms. The Police Division was headed by Charles Kowalski and accountable for the organization of patrols, watches, and lookouts. Dr. Z.R. AschenBrenner took charge of the Medical Division and was responsible for hospitals, medical supplies, and professional staff. Arnold Stolz was over the Transportation and Evacuation Division, making sure residents could safely vacate the area in case of an attack. The Publicity Division had two chiefs, Joe Himmelspach and Jim Tagg, overseeing public announcements, signs, and posters. Lastly, the Public Utility Division was co-chaired by Harry Moore and Harvey Blough and bore responsibility for water, gas, telephones, and electricity. Farmington would not be caught off guard.

Throughout the war years, there were scheduled air raids and black-out drills requiring everyone's participation. In cases of emergency, residents were advised to stay home, remain calm, and turn off the lights. They were told to shovel sand on any incendiary bomb that might hit their home, and if possible, carry it outdoors. Salvage drives were held. All metals, including buckets, wires, and tin, were collected for the assembling of tanks and trucks. Old silk and hosiery were also gathered for making gunpowder bags, parachutes, and light flares. The Red Cross sponsored the American War Relief Fund, setting up shop at the Farmington State Bank. Farmington's quota in January 1942 was $2,100.

The Methodist Church was designated an official bomb shelter. The Groves-Walker Post of the American Legion purchased cots and blankets in the event a casualty station was needed. Farmington High School served as a local Draft Center for the Selective Service System. The terminal at Kris Port was used for Civil Defense. Neighborhood War Clubs were formed to encourage the participation of each and every citizen in the war effort. The Blue Star Mothers worked hard to ensure that every single Farmington serviceman was remembered. Mr. and Mrs. Philip Henault personally organized a group that prepared packages for the soldiers overseas.

Rationing became a way of life. There were strict limits on sugar, gasoline, meat, and coffee, just to name a few. In Farmington, applications for sugar rationing books were printed in *The Farmington Enterprise*. A designated representative from each family had to disclose information such as height, weight, and eye and hair color, along with the age and sex of each household member. The doling out of sugar was somehow based upon this data. Chocolate, too, was at a premium, so whenever the Civic Theater received a shipment of Hershey bars, they sold out immediately.

As hundreds of movies were shown and thousands of tickets sold, the Civic Theater intertwined itself with the community, even hosting a wedding in early 1942. Before long, the theater blossomed into an integral part of the local war effort. Hollywood films with a patriotic flair played, along with newsreels keeping the public informed of world events. A war bond booth was built in front of the theater and scrap metal was collected. One night in 1942, as Edward Hohler sold war bonds directly onstage, Al Ross, owner of the neighboring Farmington Bakery, offered to buy a $1,000 bond if Eddie would enlist in the Marines. Hohler complied and served his country for the next three and a half years.

Hohler was not alone. Young men and women from Farmington and the surrounding township eagerly enlisted. During the war years, *The Enterprise* faithfully reported news of those who joined the military. The newspaper celebrated graduations, commissions, appointments, and heroic deeds of local sons and daughters. The paper even welcomed them home when they arrived on furlough. Barbara Ryall made front-page news when she became the first in Farmington to qualify for the Women's Auxiliary Army Corps (WAACS). She joined the ranks with her brother Jimmy, stationed in Australia, and another brother Lowell at Fort Custer.

In contrast, Private First Class Jean Lint, a Marine, made front-page news when he became Farmington's first war casualty. His parents received the dreaded news in October 1942. Their 18-year-old son was "killed in action in performance of duty for his Country" somewhere in the Pacific. Farmington men died in Okinawa, New Guinea, France, Germany, and Japan. One resident, Ray Dwyer, was killed aboard an aircraft carrier and buried at sea. Some were even lost within the borders of the United States. Captain Robert Kacy died in Glendale, California when the bomber plane he flew in crashed as it came in for a landing. Even the Warners were not exempt. Howard's son Maltby was reported missing, only to have his death later confirmed. The Coolmans lost two sons—Don and Dean. Some, like Jim Barrons, a radio operator and gunner, were taken prisoners

The Nichols School, at Thirteen Mile and Farmington Roads, operated in the early 1940s, but was burned down by vandals in December 1979. (Courtesy of the Farmington Community Library.)

Don and Dean Coolman are buried next to each other in the family's plot at North Farmington Cemetery. (Photo by Tim Ostrander.)

of war. Besides their Farmington connection, each of these young men shared one common bond—they were heroes.

Valiant deeds often made the papers as well. *The Enterprise* reported on December, 7, 1944 how Staff Sergeant Walter C. Garchow of Farmington crawled through "intense enemy machine gun and sniper fire" to assist a fallen comrade. In the midst of a heavy attack, Garchow administered first aid and pulled his friend to a safer place where he could be evacuated. Despite his gallant efforts, the wounded soldier died, but Garchow won the respect of every man who witnessed his selfless act.

Just as *The Enterprise* shared letters from the front during World War I, it also published letters from hometown boys during this war. One came from Harold Aldrich, a member of a Military Police Battalion:

> On the Anzio Beachhead, I saw more of the war at one time than I ever did before. . . . Was shelled day and night for four and a half months . . .
>
> When a bomb or shell lands extremely close to you, you can't hear it. I know that to be true because I was near (too near) a building when it was struck by a bomb . . . There was a noise, but its just a "swoosh" and that's all . . . It was so sudden and hard it took my helmet and hurled it about 20 feet in the air, blew me about 8 feet down the street, tore my

> jacket and put an egg on my head . . . I was dazed for three days . . . It is always said over here—"You never hear the one that gets you." Well, you don't hear the near misses either, you just feel 'em!

Oddly enough, there is an interesting footnote to World War II involving Farmington and one of the war's idiosyncrasies—the Japanese balloon bombs. Japan stealthily manufactured more than 9,000 of these bomb-carrying paper balloons. Hoping they would float over 6,000 miles across the Pacific, they aimed for the continental United States.

On November 3, 1944, the first of the balloon bombs were released. A few days later, a Navy patrol craft sighted what they thought was a tattered cloth floating in the Pacific about 66 miles south of San Pedro, California. Its discovery caused little concern until two weeks later when a second one was found. Within a month, these balloons were discovered as far away as Montana and Wyoming, putting national security at risk. To avoid a national panic and to prevent Japan from finding out just how far their balloons traveled, the government chose to keep what they knew to themselves.

Their plan worked for a while. Then, on May 5, 1945, a woman and five children were killed in Oregon by a balloon bomb that exploded as they dragged it from the woods. Fearing more deaths could result, the government came clean and issued a warning describing these bombs and advising all citizens not to touch them. Balloon bombs were found as far north as Alaska and as far south as Mexico. Oddly enough, one floated as far east as Michigan—Farmington, Michigan to be exact.

John T. Cook was working in his garden on Gill Road toward the end of April 1945 when he found what he thought was a tin can. Cook simply picked it up with his shovel and tossed it aside. Six weeks passed before Cook ran across that tin can again. The next day, he happened to read an article about Japanese balloon bombs. Cook decided to take a closer look at that old can. Now suspicious, he gave the object to his neighbor, William Hedt, a Michigan State Police Force sergeant. Sergeant Hedt immediately completed a formal complaint and passed it along to Army Intelligence.

Special Agent John E. Golden was sent to Farmington, where he interviewed the Cooks and the Hedts on June 15, 1945. The following is an excerpt from his reports:

> [Cook] does not know how long the object has been in his garden. The day he found it was the first day he had been working in his garden this spring. He related that neither he nor his wife at anytime heard any explosion or saw any fire in the vicinity. Cook mentioned, however, that at the time he gave the object to his neighbor, Hedt, the latter related that he and his wife thought they had seen a fire in the area where Cook found the object some months ago.

The Hedts relayed their version:

> Sometime during the latter part of March, 1945, at approximately 4 p.m. on a Sunday afternoon they were sitting in their living room. At the time Mrs. Hedt heard a muffled report similar to a shot, and happened to look out the window. She noticed a fire in an open lot, approximately three quarters of a city block, northeast of their home. Mrs. Hedt called her husband's attention to the matter and he likewise noticed the flames, but thought they were probably caused by a bonfire. According to the Hedts the fire lasted approximately three (3) minutes, and then flames were seen to spurt from the locality of the fire and Hedt thought they were similar to those which he had seen caused by magnesium. The fire then died out and the matter was forgotten until Mr. Cook gave Sergeant Hedt the object which he found in his garden.
>
> When the Hedts first saw the fire it was on the ground and gave no appearance of coming from an object hurtling through the air.

Special Agent Golden conducted a thorough search of the area and found no further evidence. A copy of his reports, as well as the mysterious tin can, were sent to Army Service Forces Headquarters, Sixth Service Command in Chicago, where it was determined that the object was identical to the lower portion of a Japanese incendiary bomb.

Japan finally surrendered on August 14, 1945, effectively ending the war. Farmington and the rest of the nation rejoiced in the Allies' victory. At last, life returned to normal. Rationing and bond drives became history. The factories in Detroit returned to automobile manufacturing while the Tigers won the World Series, beating out the Chicago Cubs.

Emerging from the depths of financial crisis and worldwide violence, a new chapter in Farmington's history was about to begin as the suburban lifestyle emerged. Location again played a pivotal role in Farmington's development as wealthy city dwellers that worked in Detroit looked to the outlying areas for a more peaceful existence. With the convenience of automobiles and the direct route on Grand River simplifying travel to and from the city, Farmington was an ideal spot. Farms were divided into country estates where professional businessmen preferring rural living to city life could build elegant homes on picturesque property. Eventually, these same country estates were split into subdivisions to accommodate even more private homes. The mayoral form of government would give way to the city manager, while the surrounding township would transform into a brand new city. Life on the farm was about to become a memory.

9. Country Estates and Subdivisions

The postwar years brought dramatic lifestyle changes to Farmington. It was a time of transformation not only for the city, but also the surrounding township. A northern Detroit suburb would soon emerge from the serene countryside. Apple orchards and dairy farms would turn into country estates before finally developing into subdivisions, spelling the end of rural life. Change and adaptation would once again play a determining factor as the city and township took on a brand new role.

As the war years came to a close, so did a local dynasty. After more than 50 years of doing business in the downtown district, Fred Cook retired. He and his partner of 37 years, Adolph Nacker, sold the general store known as Fred L. Cook and Company to Dancer's of Stockbridge, Michigan. Both well-respected businessmen and citizens of the community, the people of Farmington found it hard to say goodbye. At a party given in their honor, Floyd Nichols described the feelings of the community as reported in *The Enterprise* on January 17, 1946:

> Fred, you and Adolph have made a fine contribution to the business and civic life of Farmington, and your faces will be missed when your friends enter the old store.

At the same time, it was easy to welcome Edward Hohler home from war duty. He returned to Farmington and once again took charge of running the Civic Theater. When it was sold to Community Theatres three years later, Hohler stayed on—another stroke of luck for the community. As television moved in during the early 1950s, many theaters experienced a financial crisis. The Civic was no different and Community Theatres made the decision to close the local landmark's doors. By now, the theater was an integral part of downtown Farmington and equally important to Hohler, who came to the rescue. He bought the theater, weathering through the difficult years until the late 1950s when the novelty of television wore off and audiences gradually returned to the movies.

By 1947, the fire department was more sophisticated than ever, but fire was still a real threat. That January, the Warner block went up in flames. Putting the

Our Lady of Sorrows Church on Power and Shiawassee Roads was built on land once owned by Charles Ely. (Photo by Tim Ostrander.)

entire downtown district at risk, it was Farmington's worst fire since 1872. Both the city and the township's fire departments fought the evening blaze, but it was soon apparent that more help was needed. Redford Township, Novi, Livonia, and Northville responded to the call for help despite the sub-zero temperatures. *The Enterprise* reported the following on January 23, 1947:

> Firemen and volunteers fought the stubborn blaze for over nine hours before it was brought under control. A strong wind and heavy clouds of smoke, plus bitter cold which froze the water to ice made fighting the fire almost impossible.

When it was over, damages were estimated at $125,000 with five apartments, a beauty parlor, clothing shop, and the Farmington Post Office completely destroyed. Dickerson Hardware, the Oak Pharmacy, and eight other apartments suffered water and smoke damage.

That same year, Farmington City Cab offered 24-hour service. Patrons could ring up a taxi by calling the company at their telephone number, 2270. Delos Hamlin was mayor of Farmington, while Ernest V. Blanchard served the township as supervisor. Dickerson's Hardware boasted: "If it's Hardware—We have it!" The Burnett Brothers, William and Dan, owned a gas station on Grand River and Cass. A.C. Tagg and his son Jim were now running *The Enterprise*. During their tenure, the eight-column paper almost doubled in size from 8 pages to 14 with circulation booming from 1,000 to 4,000.

By now, there were eight churches in the area representing several denominations. Father Thomas P. Beahan was the official pastor of Our Lady of Sorrows. Through his efforts, architect Charles D. Hannan was hired and a school and an auditorium were built. Father Beahan laid the cornerstone in July 1948. By the following October, 430 children attended the new Catholic school.

That same year also brought change to the Sarah Fisher Home. With their Detroit orphanage in disrepair, the Sisters of Charity made a momentous decision. Rather than rebuilding, they consolidated the St. Vincent and Sarah Fisher Homes in what they referred to as a "children's village" located at the Farmington Hills site where they remain today.

Kris Port, still a viable airfield, experienced two plane crashes during the late 1940s. Both planes took off from the small airport only to crash in nearby fields. In 1949, an aerial photographer paid a visit and took some overhead shots of the city that were displayed in town. Local members of the Ground Observer Corps thought that Kris Port would be an ideal place for a lookout during the Cold War. They built an observation shelter that can still be seen from Orchard Lake Road. Volunteers manned the small glass edifice around the clock. No one, however, ever sighted any enemy aircraft in the vicinity. It was hard to tell whether the lookout crew felt relief or disappointment.

As the 1940s drew to a close, land value in the area increased, sending property taxes soaring. Most farmers now held jobs in the city to make ends meet while working their land part-time. Many sold large parts of their farms to wealthy businessmen who worked in Detroit, but preferred living beyond the city limits.

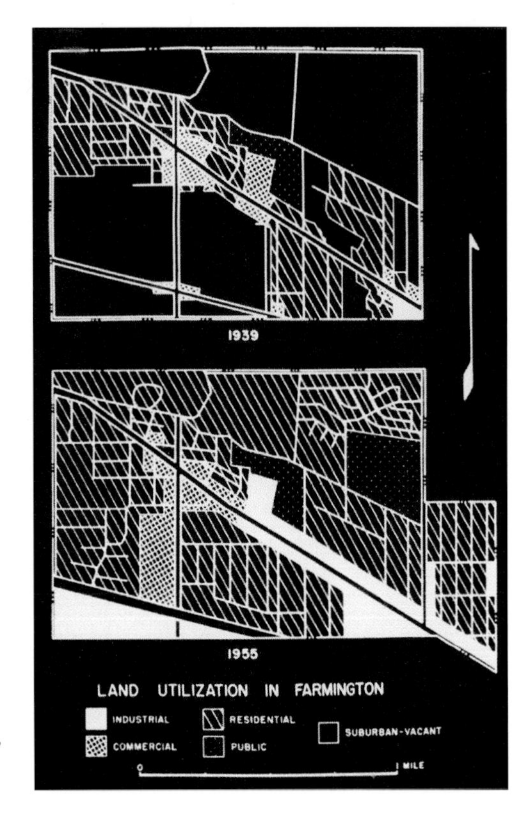

This graph compares land utilization in Farmington in 1939 and 1955. (Courtesy of the Farmington Community Library.)

Country life was appealing and, before long, Farmington and the township consisted of smaller farms nestled in between large country estates. Affluent owners of these estates often hired farmers to tend their land along with their horses. The tranquility they sought allowed the community to remain picturesque and an ideal spot for raising a family.

Men like R.K. Floyd of the Kendall Oil Company had already been living in Farmington. He purchased land, originally owned by Palmer Sherman, from the Grace family. Floyd later sold the estate to the Thompson Brown Company who developed Kendallwood Subdivision.

Attorney Edward Moseman, chairman of the Pontiac State Bank and general counsel for Standard Accident Insurance Company, also bought an estate along Farmington Road. He called it Biddestone Woods. Marcus Burrowes was once again hired to build an English-style cottage on the grounds. Moseman was an active member of the community, helping to establish the local theater group known as the Farmington Players, as well as the library. Eventually, his property was platted and Biddestone Woods was divided into a new subdivision.

The Steele property in what was once Sleepy Hollow still belonged to the Steele family. Franke Steele, grandson of Edward, built his home on Eleven Mile Road at Drake where he commuted to work in the city after World War I. The Steele land eventually became the Old Homestead Subdivision. Charles and Edna Malpass bought the Horace Green farm on Halsted Road near Minnow

This Sleepy Hollow historical marker is on Drake and Howard Roads. (Photo by Tim Ostrander.)

The Springbrook Gardens Florist on Power Road is directly across the street from Our Lady of Sorrows. (Photo by Tim Ostrander.)

Pond. Malpass, who commuted to his job as a General Motors executive, turned the farm into a country estate. Upon his retirement, William Dorman, Malpass's successor at the auto company, moved in before the land was ultimately turned into a subdivision.

The Wadenstorers sold off parts of their farm near Drake and Howard Roads to make way for country houses each sitting on 5 to 10 acres of land. The Wilcox Farm on Middlebelt and Thirteen Mile was sold and the land subdivided into the Westmont Subdivision. It later became part of Woodcreek Farms, an independent village.

The Charles Ely family once owned Springbrook Garden Farms, where horse races were held. That area, now known as the Bel Aire Subdivision, encompasses land around today's Farmington High School. The original Ely farmhouse stood where Our Lady of Sorrows Church is located on the corner of Power Road and Shiawassee. Across the street from the church is the one remaining farm building—a reconstructed barn that now houses the Springbrook Gardens Florist. The barn, originally built in 1857, was rebuilt in 1932 when Charles's daughter Imogene Ely Bickings opened the flower shop, which is still run by the family.

Farmington's first mayor Wells Butterfield and his daughter Emily—a graduate from Syracuse University and Michigan's first licensed female architect, designed Oaklands Subdivision, located at Thirteen Mile and Orchard Lake. The Butterfields first planned the Glen Oaks golf course before building homes around the fairway. Near Oaklands Subdivison was the Lock Farm, which was eventually sold to the Orchard Lake Land Company and platted into the

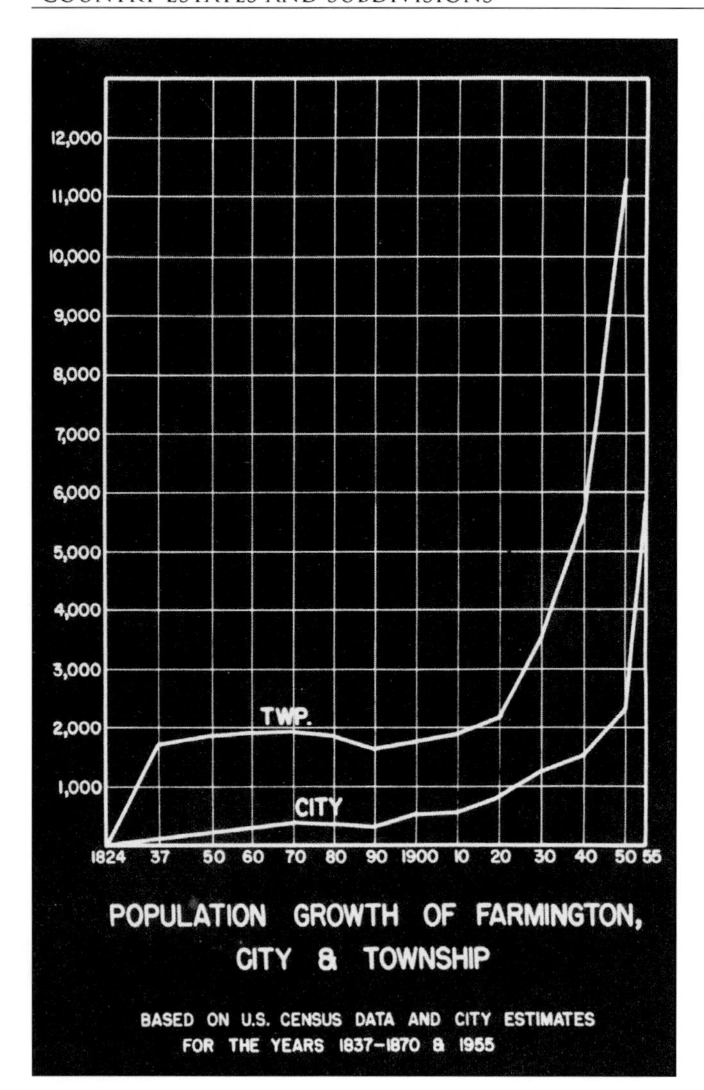

This chart shows the population growth of Farmington until 1955. (Courtesy of the Farmington Community Library.)

Pasadena Park Subdivision. A unique area, Pasadena Park was designed to reflect a Hollywood lifestyle. Even the streets were named after famous Tinseltown boulevards—Melrose, Sunset, and Hollywood. But the "lights, camera, and action" didn't last long. Shortly after World War II, the streets were renamed and the subdivision reorganized.

The 1950s brought more than a change in appearance, however. Beginning in 1951, the city government was revamped and the city charter revised. The mayoral form of management gave way to the city manager that was appointed for an indefinite term by five council members elected by popular vote. The city manager heads the administration and coordinates the various governmental departments, while the council itself is the overall governing body. They elect a mayor who presides over the council meetings and is allowed an equal vote. The city of Farmington still maintains this council-manager form of city government today.

Because Farmington Township was not yet a full-fledged city during the 1950s, the structure of its government was determined by the state of Michigan's constitution. Accordingly, the township was run by a board of trustees that included a supervisor, clerk, treasurer, and four trustees all elected by popular vote. The supervisor was considered the chief administrative officer and a voting member of the township board. The clerk acted as official record keeper and maintained the minutes of township board meetings, while the treasurer was responsible for all financial records.

As the city and the township went about their business, national affairs were in the headlines. President Harry Truman sent troops to South Korea in an attempt to keep the North Korean communists out. Under the command of General Douglas McArthur, Seoul, the South Korean capitol, was liberated on September 28, 1950. Seven months later, amidst much controversy, Truman fired McArthur and replaced him with General Matthew Ridgeway. It would be another two years before the fighting actually ended.

While Truman and McArthur were making history, the Anhut family bought the Botsford Inn. John Anhut Sr. had been in the hotel business most of his life. An admirer of Henry Ford, Anhut wasted no time in purchasing the old inn from the Fords for $225,000. To boost business, they obtained a hard-to-get liquor license and, most importantly, ingratiated themselves with the community. The Anhuts, encouraging parties, weddings, and banquets, opened the inn to everyone. The Botsford Inn was no longer the exclusive semi-private club that Henry Ford had shaped.

With a sense of adventure and a vivid imagination, the Anhuts erected a large circus tent behind the inn four years later. Known as the "Melody Circus," the tent held up to 1,800 people who came from far and wide to see live musicals, such as *Guys and Dolls*, *Gentlemen Prefer Blondes*, and *Show Boat*. No doubt, it was a colorful time in the history of the Botsford Inn.

Within ten years of World War II, residential permits rose from zero in 1944 to 478 in 1954, with three large subdivisions under construction. Major freeways opened, leading to and from Detroit. By 1955, it was estimated that 5,600 people were living in the area between dairy farms and orchards. Sixty-five percent of the locale was considered residential, 25 percent commercial, and 10 percent industrial. Traffic increased dramatically on Grand River as more and more people lived in the suburbs, but worked in Detroit. Located directly on the main thoroughfare, Farmington was an ideal spot for anyone who earned a living in Detroit, but preferred life in a more rural setting.

With the population growing, old Farmington High School, built in 1919, could no longer accommodate the increasing number of students. Therefore, in 1953, a new, larger school was erected on Shiawassee between Power and Orchard Lake Roads. Also christened Farmington High School, it replaced the old school, which was then converted into a junior high until it ultimately closed in 1976.

By 1957, the local Department of Public Safety boasted a combined fire and police department with three paid employees. They owned two fire trucks, one utility truck, and two scout cars. In case of fire, a scout car with a fire extinguisher would respond first. If the fire proved too much for the scout car, one of the fire trucks, manned by volunteers, was then summoned. The truck held 500 gallons of water and pumped up to 750 gallons per minute when connected to a fire hydrant. The days of the bucket brigade were long gone.

That same year, the Village of Wood Creek Farms incorporated—a 1 square mile area bounded by Middlebelt and Inkster between Twelve and Thirteen Mile Roads. The following year, the one and one-third square mile Village of Quakertown incorporated just north of the city. Each village was formed under the Village Home Rule Act and had a president, clerk, treasurer, assessor, and council. Despite their unique status, both villages remained part of Farmington Township.

As the 1950s drew to a close, the Detroit Red Wings won the Stanley Cup four times. Well over 1,000 homes were built in the Farmington area with another 1,000 in the works. The population more than doubled since 1940 with most of the growth occurring during the latter part of the decade. With better highways being built, more and more city people migrated to the suburbs. Farmington and the township quickly turned into a thriving metropolis as new businesses moved in and old businesses flourished.

Farmington High School is on Shiawassee between Power and Orchard Lake Roads. This photograph shows the tablet taken from the old school inside the arch. (Courtesy of the Farmington Community Library.)

North Farmington High School is on Thirteen Mile east of Farmington Road. (Courtesy of the Farmington Community Library.)

The Farmington Plaza on Grand River, the first big shopping center in the area, opened in 1957. By 1960, Kendallwood Center at Twelve Mile just east of Farmington Road opened along with the Westbrooke Center at Orchard Lake and Thirteen Mile Roads. In addition, two restaurants stood on Grand River, Ruth's Hamburger and Guffin, King of Beef. Three dentists, two doctors, and an optometrist also set up shop. Fendt Builder Supply now competed with the Union Building Supply Company. The Farmington Lumber Company vied for business with the Smith-Tupper Lumber Company. In addition, three gas stations serviced the area, while four bars and a pool hall welcomed patrons. Farmington and the township were growing by leaps and bounds.

As the district experienced unprecedented growth, they welcomed a new library, but not without a struggle. When Clinton W. Wilbur died in 1950, he left the "residue" of his estate to the city of Farmington. It was his wish that the city build either a library or a hospital with the funds. Four years later, Ruth Carlisle also bequeathed money to the city for the funding of a new library. All things considered, it took two years to decide that the money should be spent on a library, but there was another obstacle to overcome. Michigan law did not address two separate units of government working together to establish a library board. Should this be a joint venture with the township or exclusive to the city?

Wendell Brown, director of the now organized Friends of the Library, took care of the government business. Through his diligence, the Michigan state legislature passed a special act in 1955 addressing the situation. As a result, the Farmington District Library was the first such library in the state. Thanks to Brown, sharing a library is now a common practice among many communities.

The problem of location was the next hurdle, but when the U.S. Post Office moved to different quarters, the issue was resolved. The 3,800-square-foot building they vacated was refurbished and ideally suited to a formal library. Aside

Farmington Township's City Hall was built in the early 1960s on Eleven Mile and Orchard Lake Roads. (Courtesy of the Farmington Community Library.)

from a study area and lounge, the building, which was dedicated on March 2, 1959, held up to 1,800 books. Before long, however, the community knew that one library just wasn't enough. The following year, as another decade began, talk surfaced of a new library that would serve the township.

Before the second library was built, however, the new church of Our Lady of Sorrows was opened in 1961. The Farmington Historical Society was founded in 1962. A large Federal's Department Store was established downtown while some of the older buildings were renovated in the hope of invigorating the area. More farmland was subdivided into Chatham Hills, Canterbury Commons, Westwood Commons, Independence Commons, Quaker Valley, and the Franklins.

By 1963, the Downtown Farmington Center boasted 32 stores. Among them was Conroy's Super Market where butter was sold for 65¢ per pound and a dozen extra large eggs went for 59¢. Welsby House of Music sold transistor radios for $14.95 and record players for $19.95. Scott's 5&10 carried hair dryers with double lined hoods for $9.97 and 22-cup electric percolators for $8.88.

As expansion continued, local government offices of both the city and the township needed more space. The old town hall just wasn't big enough. While residents mourned the untimely death of President John F. Kennedy, the city offices built a new city hall on Liberty Street near Grand River, while the township offices relocated to a new building on Eleven Mile and Orchard Lake Roads. Once local government offices vacated the old town hall and the wrecking ball threatened the local landmark, the Masons saved the day. They chose to buy out the remaining 75 percent of the building and restore it at their own expense. Seventy-five thousand dollars later, the Masonic Temple still stands on Farmington Road as an impressive reminder of the area's rich history.

Expansion was everywhere—even the Anhuts were approached by a group of doctors wishing to purchase land behind the Botsford Inn. Their intent? To build a hospital on the site. Residents protested the idea, causing a big rift in the neighborhood. The doctors prevailed, however, and the 200-bed Botsford General Hospital (Osteopathic) was established. Toward the end of the 1960s, an apartment complex with over 100 units was also added to the grounds at a cost of $2 million.

The 1960s also brought change to LaSalle Wines and Champagne, Inc. After the death of owner Morris Twoney in 1963, the winery was sold to Chamberlin

The town hall (c. 1910) is now known locally as the Masonic Temple. (Courtesy of the Farmington Community Library.)

of America, a New York corporation. By 1966, LaSalle employed 16 full-time workers who produced 2.4 million bottles of wine, earning over $1 million in sales that year alone, but by the end of the decade, sales declined. After 37 years in business at the old DUR Powerhouse, the LaSalle Winery left Farmington and, in 1970, leased the building to the St. Julian Wine Company. Today, several offices inhabit the old building, which has become an increasingly popular place during Halloween, when the Haunted Winery offers hair-raising tours.

Farmington paused, holding its breath, during the 1964 World Olympics. That was the year that one of their own competed for the gold in Japan. Warren Jay Cawley, better know as Rex, had been a star athlete at Farmington High School during the late 1950s. In his senior year alone, he earned four gold medals in the 1959 Michigan State prep meet for the broad jump, the high hurdles, low hurdles, and running on the 880-yard relay team.

Cawley broke record after record and was actively sought after by many colleges. He settled on the University of Southern California where he continued his record-breaking habits. By 1961, he ranked first in the United States for the 400-meter hurdles, third in the 220-yard low hurdles, and fourth in the 440-yard run—no wonder they called him the "Farmington Flash." His hometown followed his collegiate accomplishments closely, but when he traveled to

Rex Cawley, 1964 Olympic Gold Medal winner, was also known as the "Farmington Flash." (Courtesy of the Farmington Community Library.)

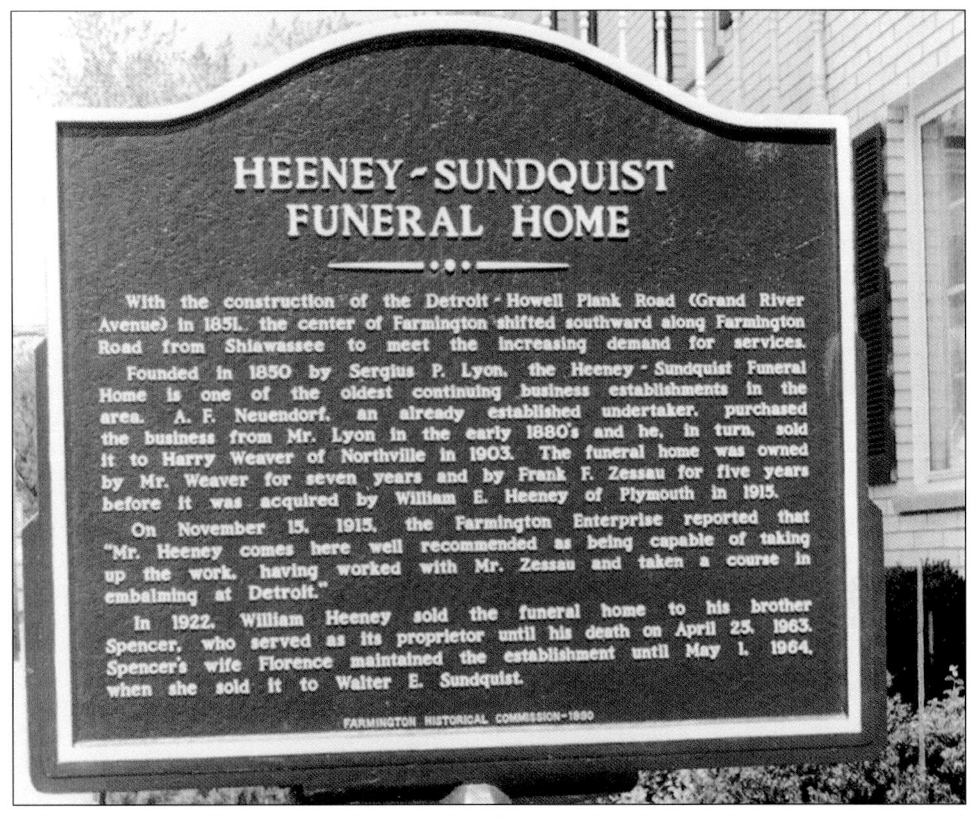

The Heeney-Sundquist Funeral Home has been in business, under various names and ownerships, since 1850. (Courtesy of the Farmington Community Library.)

Tokyo representing the United States, they really paid attention. Cawley didn't disappoint. He brought home the gold.

Another local newspaper, *The Farmington Observer*, set up shop that same year, bringing with it competition for *The Enterprise*. By now, *The Enterprise* totaled anywhere from 16 to 20 pages per issue with almost 7,000 papers being printed each week. Two years later, the two papers were combined and came to be known as *The Farmington Enterprise and Observer*.

The year 1964 also brought Walter Sundquist to town. Having been in the undertaking business for almost 20 years, he was interested in acquiring the funeral home that Sergius P. Lyon began. Since Lyon, the business had gone through several owners until William Heeney bought it in 1915. Seven years later, he sold the business to his brother Spencer. When Spencer died, Sundquist, originally from Michigan's upper peninsula, beat out 32 other undertakers and purchased the funeral home from Spencer's widow Florence. Sundquist brought Mark Ziegler on board as general manager in 1992 and made him a full partner two years later. The Heeney-Sundquist Funeral Home stands today not far from the original site of Lyon's original mortuary. Opened for business since 1850,

Harrison High School is on Twelve Mile near Middlebelt Road, and is one of three high schools that service Farmington and Farmington Hills. (Courtesy of the Farmington Community Library.)

it is considered Michigan's longest-established funeral home and serves the community along with the Thayer-Rock Funeral Home.

By 1965, the city of Farmington boasted 20 men in a combined fire and police department. Five men were on duty during each eight-hour shift, while ten volunteers rounded out the roster. There were two fire pumper trucks that could pump 750 to 1,000 gallons each minute and five patrol cars. The township's police force was also comprised of 20 officers, but the firemen were strictly volunteers and on call around the clock. Four fire stations were located throughout the township with each man serving at the fire station closest to his home. The township also owned four pumpers along with an emergency vehicle.

Between the city and the township, there were fifteen elementary schools, three junior highs, and two high schools, not including several private schools in the area. In the spring of 1964, Oakland County approved the building of a community college. A 135-acre site was chosen between Farmington Road and Orchard Lake in Farmington Township. Oakland County Community College opened its doors in 1966, offering a wide range of educational and vocational programs.

The 1960s were a controversial time of extremes, beginning with the war in Vietnam and the peace loving "Flower Children." Before the decade ended, local citizens watched in horror as the deadly 1967 riots and their aftermath swept through Detroit. The next year, however, found the same residents cheering as the Detroit Tigers brought the World Series title home. The "come-from-behind" team managed to beat the favored St. Louis Cardinals in the last of seven nail-biting games. It was a World Series to remember.

For Farmington, the decade ended in a blaze—literally. The year 1969 was when Himmelspach's Dining Room fell victim to fire. The original dairy business had turned into a family-owned restaurant located on Grand River. The fire started somewhere in the kitchen and apparently spread quickly through the ventilation system. *The Farmington Enterprise and Observer* reported the following on April 2, 1969:

> Crowds of up to 300 persons watched Himmelspach's Dining Room reduced to ashes, charred brick, and bellows of black smoke in what witnesses have called the worst fire disaster in Farmington in 20 years.
> . . . All told more than 35 firefighters fought the two-hour blaze. Farmington Township police provided crowd control and traffic assistance. No injuries were reported.

Before the fire was finally extinguished, it completely destroyed the restaurant, along with several hundred square feet of storage space. Losses totaled over $100,000.

As the war in Vietnam escalated and the 1960s ended, the 1970s began with a plan for the building of a new library. The building contract was awarded to Freeman-Darling for $1,383,556. Groundbreaking ceremonies were held on August 30, 1970 at the Twelve Mile location between Farmington and Orchard Lake Roads. Two years later, the 38,000-square-foot Farmington Public Library was dedicated.

Meanwhile, Farmington's original library held 22,000 books—4,000 more than it should have. Something had to be done. Two of three lots located at State and Liberty Streets, already owned by the city, were sold to the library for $50,000. The third lot was privately owned, but was eventually bought and, in June 1974, Freeman-Darling was once again hired to build the new 18,000-square-foot facility for $825,000. Six months later, groundbreaking ceremonies took place. On December 7, 1975, the Farmington Branch of the Farmington Community Library was dedicated.

In between the openings of both libraries, a new school was dedicated. Harrison High School, located at Twelve Mile between Orchard Lake and Middlebelt Roads, was named after retired school superintendent Gerald V. Harrison, a much-loved figure in the Farmington school system. Harrison came to Farmington from Northville in 1946 when he was offered the position of principal at the old junior-senior high school. Eleven years later, he was named superintendent and served the community well during a critical time of growth when student enrollment increased ten times over.

At the same time, the Civic Theater was also undergoing change. With an increase in attendance, it was soon apparent that the old theater needed a facelift. New front doors were installed, the restrooms tiled, and seats refurbished, but the old single-screen theater soon found itself in competition with the newer, more modern multiplexes. By the time Hohler's son Greg took over the daily operations in 1973, the Civic was once again in jeopardy.

That same year, Farmington Township, along with the villages of Quakertown and Wood Creek Farms, became the city of Farmington Hills with the blessing of township supervisor Robert McConnell. A nine-member charter commission was formed and a city charter drafted. Out of the 21 precincts, only 9 actually voted in favor of the new charter.

The Wood Creek Farms Village voted against it 340 to 131, while Quakertown Village narrowly voted it down 204 to 169. Despite the controversy, the nine precincts in favor carried the majority and, on July 1, 1973, a new city was born. Farmington Hills measured 33 square miles completely surrounding the city of Farmington and its 4 square miles. An election was held and McConnell was voted the new city's first mayor, while Floyd Cairns went from township clerk to city clerk.

As Farmington approached its sesquicentennial anniversary, daily traffic on Grand River averaged 30,000 vehicles. The school district was now spending $1,201.62 on each student. Unofficial war still raged in Vietnam. Local families were once again called upon to send their children off to battle in a distant land. As with past wars, the fighting in Vietnam took its toll on both communities. Eight neighborhood heroes who never came home are forever etched in honor on the famed wall in Washington, D.C.:

Anthony Florian Bugni, Jr.
Nathan Eugene Crouch
John William O. Groover
Henry Kolakowski, Jr.
Elzia Ray Pitcock
Thomas Frederick Riggs
Charles George Selman
Roy Kenneth Williams, Jr.

By the time the Vietnam War ended, over 12,000 people resided in the city and more than 54,000 called Farmington Hills home. Both communities combined boasted approximately 19,000 individual households and averaged between 300 and 400 new homes being built each year. The mean family income for Farmington was $18,363, while Farmington Hills families averaged slightly higher at $19,238 per year.

As the 1980s moved in, Farmington lost one of its longtime residents, Eleanor Goodenough Spicer. The land she owned was located directly on Farmington Road right next to the Longacre House, where Eleanor grew up. The Spicer farm was one of the few remaining large parcels of land in the area. Like the Longacre House, it was also originally owned by Luman Goodenough, who talked David Gray, one of his clients, into coming to Farmington from California during the summer months.

Architect Marcus Burrowes was hired once more to build a sprawling English country home. With 3-foot-thick walls, the bedrooms were located in the south end, while the dining room and kitchen were part of the north end. The panoramic view of the surrounding acres remains a breathtaking sight.

Unfortunately, Gray died in California, never making it to Farmington. Martha, his widow, sold the property, but the new owner defaulted on his loan during the Depression and the estate reverted back to Mrs. Gray. Shortly after, Eleanor Goodenough married William John Spicer. Mrs. Gray gave them the house and the property as a wedding gift. The Spicers had five children and eventually turned their country estate into a farm. When Eleanor died in 1980, her wish was that her beloved land remain untouched. The city of Farmington Hills purchased the Spicer farm and renamed it Heritage Park. The 211-acre nature preserve is a fitting tribute to the woman that lived there. Today, the entire community appreciates that panoramic view.

Three years after Eleanor Spicer's death, another piece of Farmington history was threatened. On June 27, 1983, lightning struck the 75-foot steeple of the old Salem United Church of Christ. Firefighters from both Farmington and Farmington Hills joined forces to successfully combat the flames and save the venerable church. With damages totaling $30,000, no injuries were reported, but the bats living in the belfry were left homeless.

That same year, the Red Wings drafted an 18-year-old hockey player named Stevie Yzerman. In 1984, the Tigers took center stage as they defeated the San Diego Padres, earning another World Series title. Allen Trammel and Kirk Gibson were among the favorite boys of summer. Four years later, Captain Isiah Thomas led the Detroit Pistons to their first NBA Championship when they swept the renowned L.A. Lakers in just four games.

This front view of the Spicer House in Heritage Park was home to Helen Goodenough Spicer until her death in 1980. (Photo by Tim Ostrander.)

As local sports dominated the 1980s, business at the Civic Theater was once again declining. Owner Greg Hohler took a gamble, slashing ticket prices in half from $2.50 to $1.25. As a result, the theater flourished and new projection equipment, along with a Dolby stereophonic sound system, was installed. Then, with the advent of cable television and movies on video, the theater once again floundered, forcing Hohler to take drastic action. He closed the theater for the first time in its long history. It took five weeks to extend the balcony 16 feet and incorporate a second theater with 170 seats. Adding another screen paid off and that famous marquee was saved once more.

As the 1990s began, the Pistons experienced another championship season. They beat Portland in five games, clinching the NBA title. Michigan's population was well over 9 million, making it the eighth largest state in the nation. Farmington and Farmington Hills remained affluent communities with an upward trend in professional people. The average age of Farmington's citizens was 42, while the average Farmington Hills resident clocked in at 35. Thousands of businesses both large and small dotted the area. It was a far cry from those early settlements.

By 1993, John Anhut was struggling to keep the old Botsford Inn open. He ended up selling the business to Creon Smith, who formerly ran Michigan's historic Mayflower Hotel in Plymouth. Sadly, before the decade was over, the Botsford Inn gave way to economic pressures and closed its doors.

The Civic Theater faced a similar situation. In 1999, Greg Hohler made a tough decision. He sold the Civic to the city of Farmington, who not only realized the

This image shows the old Fred Cook Building on Grand River as it looks today. (Photo by Tim Ostrander.)

theater's historic value, but also wanted to keep affordable, family entertainment in the downtown district. The city went to work updating and remodeling. An elevator was installed and a second floor showcase with its focus on Farmington history is open to the public. Today's theater, restored to its original grandeur, stands proudly, still the centerpiece of downtown Farmington.

The late 1990s found the Red Wings on a roll. The no-nonsense hockey team brought home back-to-back Stanley Cups. In 1997, they beat Philadelphia in a four-game sweep, but their celebration was cut short one week later when two team members were seriously injured in a horrific limousine crash. The careers of star defenseman Vladimir Konstantinov, affectionately known as "The Terminator," and Sergei Mnatsakanov, the team masseur, were over. Hockeytown fans everywhere, including Farmington, were devastated. Once the shock wore off, however, winning a second title became even more important. Dedicating the 1998 season to Konstantinov and Mnatsakanov, the Wings were spurred on to another Stanley Cup championship when they defeated the Washington Capitols.

As the 1990s drew to a close, taking with them the twentieth century, Farmington found itself starting a new century with 10,423 residents. Farmington Hills had a population of 82,111. Local citizens concerned themselves with "Y2K." They worried whether their utility services would be interrupted or if their computers would start. They debated over stockpiling bottled water along with canned food. Some even wondered if their cars would run. Everyone breathed a sigh of relief when January 1, 2000 came and went with little difficulty. They could not have been prepared for what happened next.

September 11, 2001 will always be remembered as one of our nation's darkest days. Much like everyone else, the citizens of both Farmington and Farmington Hills cringed in horror and disbelief as the twin towers of the World Trade Center fell and the Pentagon erupted into flames. With dust raining down on New York and smoke billowing over our nation's capitol, shock spread throughout the country. Business came to a screeching halt, schools were locked down, public events cancelled, and as news of the victims poured in, things became even more personal for local residents.

Still making history, Farmington once again mourned a loss. Forty-four-year-old Joshua Rosenthal worked as a senior vice president at Fiduciary International, Inc., whose offices were located in the World Trade Center. A successful businessman who earned his Master's degree from Princeton, Joshua's untimely death affected not only his parents, Skip Rosenthal and Alice McCoy, but the entire community. As owner of Books Abound, a popular bookstore located next to the Civic Theater, Skip Rosenthal is a familiar figure in the Farmington area. He plays a mean banjo. Perched on a wooden stool and wearing a jaunty straw hat, he often entertains the movie-going crowds who wait in line outside the old movie house. After September 11, the imposed silence in the downtown district was deafening.

In the midst of their grieving, the two cities rallied. Blood drives were held. Money and much needed supplies were collected. Multiple memorial services were conducted and, on November 11, 2001, a new marker honoring the victims was dedicated. In a poignant ceremony with the Farmington High School Marching Band playing our National Anthem, the flag was raised and the following words etched in stone were unveiled:

> In memory of those lives lost, in honor of the survivors, in appreciation for so many heroic efforts, we will never forget September 11, 2001.

Much like the rest of the nation, Farmington and Farmington Hills were forever changed after the attacks. The spirit of the original settlers, however, remains in the community. Looking to an uncertain future, residents push forward while reflecting on the past. With the widening of Farmington Road in the spring of 2002, guardrails from the DUR were uncovered, along with some of the old wooden water pipes just south of Grand River. The Salem United Church of Christ celebrated its centennial. A new state-of-the-art library opened with a specially designed Heritage Room dedicated to local history.

A new courthouse is planned for 2003. Cowley's Old Village Inn, a longstanding Irish pub located on Grand River next to the Korner Barbershop, was recently rebuilt. Several large landscape projects are in the works with trees and flowers to be planted along the main thoroughfares, ensuring that the area remains picturesque for future generations.

As the new century takes root, remembering the unique heritage of Farmington and Farmington Hills is more important than ever. The two communities can be proud of the past that unites them, as they look ahead and continue what those early settlers started. North Farmington High School graduate Scott B. Terrill summed it up nicely when he wrote the winning theme for Farmington's 150th birthday celebration: "Pride In Our Past—Faith In Our Future."

Arthur Power would be pleased.

Bibliography

Primary Sources

Nathan Power's Diary, 1824–1874.

Secondary Sources

City of Farmington Hills Historic District Commission, The. *Farmington Hills Historic District*. Michigan, 2001.

Clifton, James A. *Indians of North America, The Potawatomi*. New York: Chelsea House Publishers, 1987.

Dunbar, Willis Frederick. *Michigan: A History of the Wolverine State*. Michigan: William B. Eerdmans Publishing Company, 1965.

———. *Michigan Through the Centuries, Volume I*. New York: Lewis Historical Publishing Company, Inc., 1955.

Durant, Samuel W. *History of Oakland County Michigan*. Philadelphia, PA: L.H. Everts and Company, 1877.

Farmington/Farmington Hills Historic Homes, Newspaper Articles. Binder Compiled at the Farmington Community Library. November 1990.

———. *From Ice Age to Space Search, Farmington: An Original Entity, Being The Natural History of Farmington.* Farmington: Farmington Hills Historical Commission, 1976.

Farmington History, Excerpts from Newspapers, Articles and Pamphlets. Binder compiled at the Farmington Community Library.

Fox, Jean M. *Farmington Centennial Families, Volume III*. Farmington: Farmington Hills Historical Commission, 1978.

———. *Fred M. Warner Progressive Governor*. Farmington: The Farmington Hills Historical Commission, 1988.

———. *Letters from 1860: The Howards of Farmington*. Farmington: The Farmington Hills Historical Commission, 1994.

———. *More Than a Tavern: 150 Years of Botsford Inn*. Farmington: The Botsford Inn, 1986.

Fuller, George N., ed. *Historic Michigan, Land of the Great Lakes, Volume II*. Lansing,

MI: National Historical Association, Inc., 1924.
Golden, Brian M. *Farmington Junction, A Trolley History*. Lansing, MI: 1999.
Graham, Clyde. *Memories of North Farmington*. Farmington: The Farmington Hills Historical Commission, 1999.
Knighton, Burton S. "The Changing Function of Farmington, Michigan." Typewritten report. Detroit, 1955.
May, George S. *Michigan and the Civil War Years 1860–1866 A Wartime Chronicle.* Lansing, MI: Michigan Civil War Centennial Observance Commission, 1964.
Millbrook, Minnie Dubbs, ed. *Twice Told Tales of Michigan and Her Soldiers in The Civil War.* Lansing, MI: Michigan Civil War Centennial Observance Commission, 1966.
Moehlman, Ruth Roth. *If Walls Could Talk, Heritage Homes of Farmington.* Farmington: The Farmington Hills Historical Commission, 1993.
Peel, Lee S. *Farmington: A Pictorial History.* Michigan, 1993.
Pentecost, Paul. "John Clem, the Drummer Boy of Shiloh." *Detroit News.* 2 February 1961.
Powell, Suzanne. *The Potawatomi*. New York: Franklin Watts, Division of Grolier Publishing, 1997.
Robert B. Cook Collection. "Some Early Families of Farmington, Michigan." Binder compiled by Vayle Lorion, 1961.
Silliman, Sue Imogene. *Michigan Military Records.* Baltimore, MD: Genealogical Publishing Company, 1969.
Strye, Stella. *The Religious History of Farmington*. Farmington: The Farmington Hills Historical Commission, 1978.

This view of Oakland Street near downtown Farmington depicts the Salem United Church of Christ with a neighboring cornfield, c. 1920. (Courtesy of the Farmington Community Library.)

INDEX